D0856103

PERSPECTIVES IN ARTIFICIAL INTELLIGENCE
Volume I: Expert Systems
Applications and Technical Foundations

ELLIS HORWOOD SERIES IN ARTIFICIAL INTELLIGENCE

Joint Series Editors: Professor JOHN CAMPBELL, Department of Computer Science, University College London, and
Dr JEAN HAYES MICHIE, Knowledgelink Limited, Edinburgh

* *In preparation*

PERSPECTIVES IN ARTIFICIAL INTELLIGENCE
Volume I: Expert Systems Applications and Technical Foundations

Editors:

J. A. CAMPBELL
Department of Computer Science, University College London

J. CUENA
Laboratorio de Sistemas Inteligentes
Universidad Politécnica, Madrid, Spain

ELLIS HORWOOD LIMITED
Publishers · Chichester

Halsted Press: a division of
JOHN WILEY & SONS
New York · Chichester · Brisbane · Toronto

First published in 1989 by
ELLIS HORWOOD LIMITED
Market Cross House, Cooper Street,
Chichester, West Sussex, PO19 1EB, England
The publisher's colophon is reproduced from James Gillison's drawing of the ancient Market Cross, Chichester.

Distributors:

Australia and New Zealand:
JACARANDA WILEY LIMITED
GPO Box 859, Brisbane, Queensland 4001, Australia

Canada:
JOHN WILEY & SONS CANADA LIMITED
22 Worcester Road, Rexdale, Ontario, Canada

Europe and Africa:
JOHN WILEY & SONS LIMITED
Baffins Lane, Chichester, West Sussex, England

North and South America and the rest of the world:
Halsted Press: a division of
JOHN WILEY & SONS
605 Third Avenue, New York, NY 10158, USA

South-East Asia
JOHN WILEY & SONS (SEA) PTE LIMITED
37 Jalan Pemimpin # 05–04
Block B, Union Industrial Building, Singapore 2057

Indian Subcontinent
WILEY EASTERN LIMITED
4835/24 Ansari Road
Daryaganj, New Delhi 110002, India

© **1989 J.A. Campbell and J. Cuena/Ellis Horwood Limited**

British Library Cataloguing in Publication Data
Perspectives in artificial intelligence. —
(Ellis Horwood series in artificial intelligence).
Vol. 1, Expert systems: applications and technical foundations
1. Artificial intelligence
I. Campbell, J. (John)   II. Cuena, J. (Jose)   III. Series
006.3
Library of Congress Card No. 89–1819

ISBN 0–7458–0659–7 (Ellis Horwood Limited)
ISBN 0–470–21434–1 (Halsted Press)

Printed in Great Britain by Hartnolls, Bodmin

Table of contents

Foreword

When the Basque Government decided in 1985 to hold the Second World Basque Congress, it was because it had become conscious of a need within modern Basque society: a need to review the present situation of that society and to discuss thoroughly the present reality in order to prepare for the future. It was clear that an essential element of the preparation would have to be the study of the current state of many relevant academic and scientific subjects.

The complex and enriching organizational stages now lie behind us. The Congress has taken place; for us it has been an unprecedented academic experience, an incomparable show of collaboration and mutual contribution to international scientific culture, and a great communication effort which has had the effect of turning a thousand experts from all over the world who have visited us for the different conferences within the Congress into special ambassadors for Euzkadi.

In this context the Second World Basque Congress still has two final aims to fulfil. The first is to form the nucleus of a new Basque scientific organization, to channel the gains from this experience towards a future rich in ideas. The second is to disseminate widely the contents of all the invited and contributed papers from the thirty-four conferences of the Congress, to ensure that the corresponding study and debate of a wide range of scientific and social problems affecting the world today reaches the widest possible audiences and therefore has the greatest possible value.

For the second of these two phases the Basque Government is supporting a twofold effort:

(a) To make its own publication summarizing the transactions of all of the conferences of the Congress, and hence to sum up the effect of the Congress itself.

(b) To encourage the organizers of each conference to publish for world-wide circulation the detailed scientific records of their work and the work of their international collaborators, by establishing contact with relevant publishing companies and other institutions specializing in the different disciplines. This is precisely the context of the present two-volume work, which has arisen from the conference on artificial intelligence.

I am sure that, by lending our support to this enterprise, we shall have achieved our basic goals of making a distinctively Basque contribution to international scientific work in the areas of the conferences and of sowing the necessary seeds in Euzkadi which will give hope and concrete scientific support to a new social order in its future development.

José Antonio Ardanza
President of the Basque Government

Preface

The following publication is a collection made from among the invited and contributed papers presented at the Conference on Artificial Intelligence, held in Donostia-San Sebastián between 7 and 11 September 1987, within the framework of the Second World Basque Congress. This Congress was sponsored by the Basque Government and was made up of thirty-four different conferences within a wide range of scientific subjects, chosen for their significance in current international research and for their interest and ability to contribute to the future progress of Basque society.

For the conference on artificial intelligence, we have chosen to cover a wide range of topics (expert systems, natural language, reasoning techniques, . . .), in order to obtain a reasonable survey of present active areas of the subject, and to aim for a coverage that pays proper attention both to basic research and to examples of specific applications of methods of artificial intelligence. The contributors to the conference have been selected accordingly.

The importance of artificial intelligence as a driving force for developments in computer science and many other subjects that make direct or indirect use of computer-based technology is undeniable. This is one reason for the inclusion of artificial intelligence within the list of topics for conferences of the Congress. Clearly a rapidly-developing society such as Euzkadi must ensure that its own scientists and technologists are educated as thoroughly as possible in such a crucial topic, and that its educators and researchers become familiar with the latest advances and the latest perspectives available internationally. The present volumes are a convincing record of the significant step forward which was achieved by means of the conference. We expect that they will have equal value to readers in similar situations in other countries, and that they will serve as a tangible Basque contribution to international scientific activity.

Luis Gurrutxaga
Secretary General of the Second World Basque Congress

Introduction

As the preface to the first volume states, the origin of the collection of articles that makes up this two-volume set was the conference on artificial intelligence (AI) within the Second World Basque Congress in September 1987. The purpose of the conference was to survey developments in AI that were of particular value for those people already teaching in advanced computer science or concerned with the development of industrial enterprises using advanced computer science, in the Basque country. The organizers had this audience in mind when they outlined their programme and issued invitations to speakers. As a consequence, the collection is of potential value to similar audiences elsewhere: the scientific contents of the articles are obviously not tied to particular national surroundings.

Collections that cover relatively large areas within AI usually belong in one of two classes: proceedings of general conferences like IJCAI or AAAI, or surveys that start from the work of a single laboratory (e.g. Winston and Brown, 1979) or that approximate the ideal of a single-author textbook (Yazdani, 1986). The present volumes do not fit neatly into any of these classifications. The differences are not accidental. The primary reason is that the AI conference of the Basque World Congress was intended to include both invited survey papers, setting out points of view on some basic issues, and research-level contributions which could give an audience (containing university faculty members in computer science, graduate students and interested technical staff from appropriate companies) an exposure to research issues without demanding any extensive experience in carrying out that research. The present volumes have been compiled with exactly this type of audience in mind: they give a post-introductory view of AI which should also be an effective bridge between the levels of basic AI texts and proceedings of IJCAI, AAAI and single-topic AI research conferences. This type of bridge is not yet as common as it deserves to be, in the published AI literature.

These volumes do not attempt to take up all the topic-headings that appear in indexes to basic AI textbooks. Instead, there is a conscious bias in the choice of subjects towards issues that have not got the past attention that they deserve or are likely to occupy more of the central stage in AI in the future. These predictions do not come from some infallible oracle; they are expressions of various opinions from the people who planned the programme of the conference and some of the invited speakers. One of the benefits of taking part in a conference in such capacities is that one can express subjective prejudices about the lessons of the past and bets on the future. In AI, there is still room both for subjective opinions and for formulae drawn up by committees of trainee elder statesmen.

The invited material that begins the first volume covers topics that fit the description just given. 'Expert systems' takes the first place here, because expert systems were responsible for the initial commercial successes of AI and are still by far the most heavily exploited products of AI technology. Despite their successes, however, or perhaps *because* of the limits to their successes throughout the 1980s, most present expert systems are perceived as failing to be enough like real experts in their behaviour to please the most demanding or experienced customers. There are several manifestations of this failing: for example, a lack of flexibility or human-oriented facilities for *automated explanation* of the outputs of the systems, and (possibly one reason why the level of explanation is most often less than satisfactory) limited or no mechanisms to connect standard rule-based surface knowledge of a subject with typical human experts' deeper knowledge of that subject, based on concepts like models that can justify or at least give some support to the surface rules. One phrase used to describe the research field whose objective is to correct those defects is 'second-generation expert systems'. This is the subject of the first invited article. Another way to look at the same subject in this book is simply as an update on what has been happening in research to improve the quality of AI's most mature or exportable current technology.

Learning is a long-lived issue in AI. It will be with us as long as AI exists as a scientific activity. The obvious reason for this interest is that non-artificial intelligence and learning are inseparable. In fact, there are schools of thought which say that the latter is the best specific evidence for the former. Inside AI, there are similar schools of thought — visible if not necessarily heavily populated — which prefer to regard nothing as *real* AI unless some component of machine learning is involved. Fortunately there is no shortage of sources on machine learning in the AI literature (Michalski *et al.*, (1983, 1986). The relevant contribution to the present volumes therefore takes the chance to make a point that deserves more attention than it has received in the past: that analogical methods are likely to be significant in future AI. This prediction is a good one because 'analogy' has prospects of being useful in two rather different sub-fields of AI: reasoning and learning. In the language of horse racing, 'analogy' is a good bet for AI because it is an each-way bet. The coverage of the subject in the present collection is good source material for readers who want to be informed, or to calculate the odds.

The survey articles in the first volume conclude with a subjective view of computer architectures that are likely to be helpful for work in AI. This is a topic which will have an increasing importance in the future as the choice of different commercially-available architectures widens. The starting-point for the discussion is the assertion that serious knowledge-based computing must make serious use of both pointers and parallelism, because these ideas are inherent in the processing of knowledge. This is not to say that the pointers and parallelism available in typical experimental computer architectures in 1988 have much to do with the same ideas in applied cognition. However, starting from this emphasis is a good way to distinguish between computer architectures that are likely to be useful for AI applications in the future and those that are not.

The remainder of the first volume concentrates on AI applications. Not surprisingly, this means that expert systems or rule-based systems come in for most of the attention. Because of the very wide range of these applications, one can try either to cover the whole range thinly with different samples or to concentrate. We have used the second option here. The areas that receive special attention are design and decision support. They have both been recognized for some time as being well suited to the use of rule-based systems, since many of their component pieces of knowledge are heuristic and natural to express in rules, but they have not been treated so thoroughly in print as other areas of application like diagnosis, planning or administrative law.

The second volume has two main focuses: natural language, and improvements in the use of databases by AI methods. It begins with a topic that clearly belongs to natural-language processing rather than any other part of AI, but that is not often seen in published material on AI: machine translation. The traditional separation between translation and natural-language processing in AI is a matter of history, as historical surveys like those of Hutchins (1986) show. But the aims of the subjects have enough of an overlap that people working on each subject should not ignore what is happening in the other one. For this reason the conference has included some up-to-date views of machine translation that are difficult to find elsewhere in the AI literature. Articles on natural-language processing from a more traditional AI viewpoint then follow, including one novelty (though perhaps not so novel for a Basque conference): an article dealing with aspects of processing problems for the Basque language.

The common theme of the articles in the second volume is human–computer interaction where the AI component is intended to react primarily to the special needs of the user rather than to the special features of some application area. One of these special needs is for interaction with collections of data without having to be trained in how to run database programs. The section of the second volume that deals with the coupling between expert systems and databases shows something of the achievements of European research in this direction, and reinforces a point that has been made elsewhere (Campbell, 1987): that, while this area is of world-wide research interest, it is a particular European speciality.

The second volume ends with some coverage of a further human-oriented application that receives plenty of exposure in its own specialized conferences but is not often enough treated in general surveys of AI applications: computer-aided instruction.

The intention of the organizers of the AI conference in the Second World Basque Congress was to provide a survey which could not touch on every subject under the current umbrella of AI but which would present a representative picture of research in a coherent set of topics. This set is one that travels well, like robust wine. It does not require heavy investment in equipment or extensive existing software in order to make progress in the subjects treated here, and any such progress in research is likely to have immediate applications in places that do not have the same economic and technological advantages as Massachusetts or California. This is clearly relevant to the Basque country, Euzkadi, but it is probably equally relevant to readers in a majority of states in the USA, not to mention other countries. We are therefore pleased to offer this collection to an international audience.

REFERENCES

Campbell, J. A. (1987) Applications of artificial intelligence within the ESPRIT programme. In W. Brauer and W. Wahlster (eds), *Wissensbasierte Systeme,* Springer-Verlag, Berlin, pp. 373–379.

Hutchins, W. J. (1986) *Machine Translation: Principles and Applications,* Ellis Horwood, Chichester.

Michalski, R. S., Carbonell, J. and Mitchell, T. (eds) (1983, 1986) *Machine Learning: an Artificial Intelligence Approach,* Springer-Verlag, Berlin, vol. 1 (1983); vol.2 (1986).

Winston, P. H. and Brown, R. H. (1979) *Artificial Intelligence: an MIT Perspective,* MIT Press, Cambridge, MA.

Yazdani, M. (ed.) (1986) *Artificial Intelligence: Principles and Applications,* Chapman & Hall, London.

Part I
Fundamentals

1

The deepening of expert systems

Luc Steels,
VUB AI-LAB,
Pleinlaan 2, 1050 Brussels, Belgium

1. INTRODUCTION

Since its conception in the early 1970s through the work on DENDRAL (Feigenbaum *et al.*, 1971) and MYCIN (Shortliffe, 1976), the notion of an expert system has swept the world and captured the imagination of computer technologists and users alike. The success of the concept of an expert system can no longer be denied. It points out that there is a large demand in the computer user community for user-friendly, intelligent-looking computer systems and for systems that tackle problems requiring reasoning. After some hesitation we see solid projects emerging in many organizations and we already see a number of successful applications, even though it takes at least several man-years to develop a serious system.

Despite this positive outlook, there are also some negative trends. The most troublesome one is that the notion of expert system is increasingly being trivialized, leading to false user expectations and superficial results. The first part of the chapter focuses on this trend. The second part reviews the counteracting trend towards 'deeper' expert systems that utilize richer representations of the domain instead of the shallow heuristic rules which formed the exclusive basis of first-generation expert systems.

2. WHAT ARE EXPERT SYSTEMS?

Given the confusion still surrounding expert systems, it is not entirely superfluous to discuss first in more detail what expert systems are. Basically there appear to be four essential characteristics:

(1) An expert system is a computer program *designed to assist the human expert in a limited but difficult real-world domain*. It not only helps in computation-related tasks such as numerical calculation or information retrieval but also in the tasks which require reasoning. The domain must be difficult in the sense that only a human who is 'expert' in the domain can solve the problem. Expert systems are seldom there to replace a human expert. To carry out a dialogue with systems such as MYCIN (Shortliffe,

1976) or the Dipmeter Advisor (Smith, 1984) or to understand their results, one must already be quite an expert. Expert systems are therefore mainly intended to raise levels of expertise or to make sure that the expert does not overlook something (cf. the use of a pocket calculator by people who know perfectly well how to calculate).

(2) The reasoning of an expert system is *modelled after the reasoning of a human expert.* We could write a program for medical diagnosis based on statistical correlations over large samples of medical records. Although such a program would solve a difficult real world problem requiring expertise, it does not solve it based on a model of the human expert. Because expert systems are modelled after human experts it follows that in the *best* case they match the performance of the human expert.

(3) An expert system not only has representations dealing with the domain but also *keeps representations of itself: of its internal structure and functioning.* It therefore has limited forms of self-knowledge. Ordinary programs can run and produce results but they have no explicit accessible representation of themselves at run-time, nor do they keep a record of what and why they did something. Explicit self-representations make explanations how a problem was solved possible. They also make dynamic extensions possible for example through interaction with the expert.

(4) The interface is designed using restricted forms of natural language or graphical interaction, so that *the expert system is directly usable by the expert.* This contrasts with many computer applications which require the use of a specialized language.

3.   PROBLEMS WITH EXPERT SYSTEMS

3.1   Trivialization

Although the first examples of expert systems clearly satisfy the above criteria, there is a tendency by developers of expert systems and many companies in the business of supplying tools to trivialize the idea to get their message (i.e. product) through. 'Expert system' is increasingly becoming another word for 'computer program'. The domains of application have become simpler and simpler, no longer requiring the intervention of top experts who have had years of training and years of expertise. Many expert systems are no longer constructed after a careful empirical observation of human experts. They can no longer be said to embody serious reasoning but follow instead a set of decision steps which is completely determined in advance, just like an algorithm. Many systems have no longer a serious model of their own program. This drastically reduces their power for explanation or dynamic extension.

The trivialization of expert systems has led to a number of problems such as:

(1) *False user expectations:* The impression has been given that all problems in constructing expert systems are solved and that any type of expertise can be turned into an expert system with little effort (if only you buy the tool or consulting time from the company in question!).

(2) *False programmer expectations:* A mass of people have entered the field recently often with not much more know-how than obtainable from a tutorial or from reading one of the superficial books on the subject that now flood the market.

(3) *Underestimation of resources:* When these programmers after having been baptized (or having baptized themselves) knowledge engineers start their projects, they are given extremely limited resources, both in time and in computer power (e.g. a shell on a PC). In particular, the effort required from the expert is usually far underestimated.

(4) *Superficiality of results:* One side effect is that many expert systems are hardly worthy of the name. Although such systems have absorbed some concepts or techniques from AI (e.g. rule-based or logic programming, interactive natural-language-like interface, etc.) the problems they solve could just as well be solved using standard programming techniques.

(5) *Loss of interest by AI community:* Because of the trivialization of expert systems, the AI community, which is supposed to be doing the fundamental research, feels no longer associated with expert systems and sees knowledge engineering as just a fancier word for programming. One consequence is that the theories behind expert systems development have for the most part stagnated since the mid-1970s and (worse) that the knowledge of experts which forms the core of expert systems is only rarely studied from a scientific point of view.

This process of trivialization, triggered by a drive to make money as quickly as possible, is unfortunate. There is a real danger that people lose interest as quickly as expert systems come into prominence. This is unfortunate in the sense that the notion of an expert system and the techniques developed for building them do constitute a significant and important advance in computer technology. It is unfortunate for AI becuase it would lose an opportunity for the application and real world testing of its insights. In the end it will hurt the expert system business community because the trivialization makes them less necessary.

3.2   Weak foundations

There are also serious problems in knowledge engineering. First of all there is a variety of techniques known in AI (e.g. the different control regimes of inference engines: forward, backward, depth-first, breadth-first, hill-climbing, explicit control, and so on). However, there is no theory on when a particular technique has to be selected. Commercial shells incorporate particular choices but do not tell their users what these choices are good for; in fact, they advertise that the shell is good for everything.

Second there is too much emphasis on the implementation aspect. Constructing an expert system is often viewed as a matter of programming in an AI language. However, a sorting program written in a rule-based language or in a logic-programming language does not become an expert system in sorting! What is lacking is a serious analysis at the knowledge level, i.e. an implementation-independent investigation of the knowledge structures and problem solving strategies used by the expert.

4.   MOTIVATION FOR DEEPER EXPERT SYSTEMS

Expert systems are based on a model of the human expert, so an important task in their construction is an extensive investigation of the knowledge of the human expert. The first impression one gets during such an investigation is that the expert utilizes a large collection of rules, together with other structures defining objects and properties that participate in the rules. Consequently expert system developers focus on the extraction and implementation of these rules and building expert systems has become almost synonymous with building rule-based systems.

Clancey (1979) was one of the first researchers to start looking 'behind the rules'. His research was motivated by the construction of educational tools based on expert systems. He discovered quickly that the MYCIN rule base is too weak as a representation of the expert knowledge for teaching situations. Other researchers, such as Swartout (1981), were motivated by a need for better explanation facilities. Expert systems do provide explanations but they are weak in the sense that they can only report back the rules that have been used. More adequate explanations would require the system knowing something about the rationale behind the rules.

Another motivation for studying in more depth expert knowledge comes from the problem of building them. It is well known that knowledge acquisition is a difficult process. The expert's rules are usually incomplete, particularly on a first pass. They may even be inconsistent. A rule base tends to become unstable when its size goes beyond the explicit comprehension of the designers. Moreover, the boundaries during development are unclear. It is very difficult to say how much of a particular field a specific system matters. Several researchers such as Wielinga and Breuker (1984) have been studying expert knowledge in depth in an attempt to develop a more solid methodology for knowledge acquisition. This has also yielded new insights into the deeper forms of knowledge used by experts.

Other researchers have been looking at the automatic acquisition of expert knowledge through machine learning. One way to do this is by induction (Michalski, 1983). This requires, however, a large set of example cases and will only yield the rules themselves, without any rationale or deeper understanding. An alternative approach is to use deeper forms of knowledge as generators of rules. An early example of this work is Mitchell (1978) whose LEX program is capable of deriving heuristic rules in the domain of symbolic integration. Another example is META-DENDRAL (Buchanan and Mitchell, 1978) which induced rules about mass spectrum analysis similar to the rules used in the DENDRAL expert system.

It is significant that although the motivations of these researchers are different they have all basically arrived at similar models of what expert knowledge looks like. The main insight is that rules are clearly used by experts *but* that the rules form only the top layer of the expert's knowledge. Consequently they are sometimes referred to as *surface knowledge*. Complemented by the rules other structures are found which can be decomposed in two types: domain theories and problem solving knowledge (in the sense of knowledge about how to solve problems in general). They constitute the *deep knowledge*. The relation is expressed in the following equation:

$$\text{domain theory} + \text{problem solving knowledge} = \text{heuristic rule}$$

In other words, heuristic rules are the result of applying or specializing problem solving knowledge to domain theories. The next section elaborates this framework.

5.   THE NATURE OF DEEP KNOWLEDGE

Problem-solving knowledge consists for the most part of general strategies for handling the application of knowledge to real world situations. The strategies deal with organizing and restricting search, avoiding questions or observations that are not absolutely necessary, dealing with uncertainty, inconsistency, incompleteness of evidence, etc. There is a range of such strategies. Some of them are relatively domain-specific or specializations of general strategies (e.g. divide and conquer) to a domain (e.g. diagnosis). Others are completely general, e.g. 'make easy observations first'. Clancey and Letsinger (1981) looked for example at a rule like that in Fig. 1. They

IF: 1) The infection is meningitis
    2) The subtype of meningitis is bacterial
    3) Only circumstantial evidence is available
    4) The patient is at least 17 years old
    5) The patient is an alcoholic
THEN: There is suggestive evidence that diplococcus-pneumoniae is an organism causing the meningitis

Fig. 1 — MYCIN rule illustrating various problem solving strategies.

noticed that hidden in the rule is a top-down refinement strategy. Is there an infection? Is it meningitis? Is it bacterial? Is it diplococcus-pneumoniae? This strategy is not explicitly represented, nor is the supporting knowledge (such as *Diplococcus pneumoniae* is an organism related to bacterial meningitis). This leads to weak explanations but also to a weak methodology in knowledge acquisition, e.g. it was probably overlooked that there are other intermediate categories of meningitis (such as acute–chronic meningitis). A second strategy hidden in the rule is to eliminate hypotheses based on easily-accessible evidence. In this case, children are not alcoholic so clause 4 acts as a screening rule for the alcoholism test. Again, the program does not have an explicit representation about the relation between

age and alcoholism, nor does it have an explicit representation of the
screening strategy.

The top-down refinement strategy and the screening strategy are examples of control strategies. They are concerned with the organization and
restriction of search. However, there are many other sorts of strategies as
well. The rule in Fig. 2, also from MYCIN, illustrates a strategy to deal with
incompleteness. At first reading, this rule appears obscure until we understand that the underlying strategy is a specific case of default reasoning: not
knowing whether p is true may allow you to conclude that not p is true.

IF: It is not known whether there are factors that interfere with the patient's
      normal bleeding
THEN: It is definite (1.0) that there are not factors that interefere with the
      patient's normal bleeding.

Fig. 2 — MYCIN rule illustrating default strategy.

It turns out that the rules found in expert systems all have one or more
such hidden strategies. The surface knowledge therefore constitutes a form
of compiled knowledge: part of the domain theory is transformed according
to a particular strategy into a heuristic rule.

Within this framework we can also see what domain theories look like.
They are typically networks of structured descriptions. The descriptions
deal with the objects of the domain (e.g. diseases, symptoms, laboratory
tests, patients, etc.) Relations in the network are specialization relations
(used e.g. for implementing top-down refinement), causal relations (e.g. for
implementing principled diagnostic strategies), associative relations (for
formulating hypotheses), etc. Part of the domain theory underlying MYCIN
is a taxonomy of diseases of which Fig. 3 contains a small portion relevant for
the previous example (from Clancey and Letsinger, 1981).

Domain theories may also be in the form of rules. An example is given in
Fig. 7. Note that the domain theories are typically not principled models of
the domain, e.g. scientific theories or qualitative versions of it (Hobbs and
Moore, 1985), but abstractions and heuristic approximations.

The discussion of an expert system for diagnosis of circuits in Davis
(1982) illustrates the same point for another application domain. A typical
strategy in diagnosis is progressive restriction. Observations are made which
allow diagnosis to focus on a subpart of the system.

For example, given the circuit in Fig. 4, we may have heuristic rules of
the sort contained in Fig. 5. These heuristic rules compile the problem
solving strategy of progressive restriction to a subcircuit. The domain theory
in this case consists of the network of causal relations describing the circuit.
We found essentially the same problem-solving strategy when building an
expert system for train diagnosis although the kinds of causal relations and
type of technical system are very different (De Wael, 1987).

Other expert systems can be analysed in the same way. For example, R1
(McDermott, 1980) basically follows a strategy of repairing almost-right

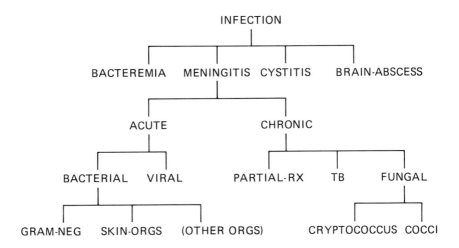

Fig. 3 — Part of the disease hierarchy underlying MYCIN.

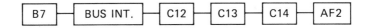

Fig. 4 — Example circuit used by Davis.

IF The signal is OK at B7 and
    the signal is blocked at AF2
THEN the signal is being lost somewhere between B7 and AF2

IF the signal is OK at B7 and
    the signal is blocked at C12
THEN the signal is being lost somewhere between B7 and C12

Fig. 5 — Example rules for diagnosing circuit.

solutions. The system has a large collection of templates which describe
partial solutions and its rules will refine and complete the partial solution to
adapt it to the problem situation.

6.   IMPACT ON EXPERT SYSTEM CONSTRUCTION

Given these insights we can now look at what difference they make for building expert systems. The first impact is on the methodology for constructing them. This is discussed in this section. The next section looks at the impact on architecture.

From the viewpoint of a deeper model of expertise, it is clearly inappropriate to approach the expert with questions of the sort 'what are your rules'. Instead a richer set of models for interpreting the problem-solving behaviour of the expert, as for example observed through protocols, can be developed.

An example of this approach is the KADS methodology and support system (Breuker and Wielinga, 1985). In this methodology, the first main goal is the identification of the deep knowledge of the expert: the domain theories and the strategies. The domain theories are in the form of models (causal, process models, formal models), structures (such as sub or super-class, part or whole), and so on. The strategies describe explicitly the problem solving strategy underlying concrete heuristic rules.

One important aspect of the analysis is to identify clearly the epistemological status and role of each element in the reasoning process. For example, it is made explicit whether a particular property will serve as a symptom and what the role of the sympton is going to be in a strategy (e.g. yield evidence, trigger an hypothesis). Another property might be identified as a cause, whose role is the support of a particular empirical association. A scheme describing the various types of elements involved and their respective role in the problem-solving process is called the conceptual structure (Bennett, 1983).

KADS supports knowledge engineering in two ways. On the one hand it provides a catalogue of general interpretation models which can be used to approach classes of domains. For example, many applications in diagnosis tend to use the same conceptual structures (involving symptoms, factors, causes, subsystems) and the same problem-solving strategy (such as the progressive restriction strategy discussed earlier). Second it provides a collection of software tools. For example, there are data structures for representing conceptual structures, problem-solving strategies, etc., and tools to refine these interactively or to relate them to verbal data. Other systems have been built along similar lines.

7.   IMPACT ON EXPERT SYSTEM ARCHITECTURE

The distinction between deep and shallow knowledge does not necessarily imply another architecture for expert systems. We could implement only the heuristic rules and leave the deep knowledge sketched out on paper. A first step is to make the underlying strategic structure of a rule explicit. Such a technique was used for example by Lenat (1983) in EURISKO. However, we can go a lot further and represent the deep knowledge as well as the interactions between deep and shallow knowledge explicitly as well. This is the idea behind second-generation expert systems (Steels, 1984).

A second-generation expert system has an explicit representation of the deep knowledge. There is a component containing the domain theories and one containing the problem solving knowledge. Typically there is also a component containing shallow knowledge in the form of rules, which are compilations of the application of deep knowledge for a class of situations. This component is used to speed up the whole system. The derivation of adequate rules from deep knowledge is a non-trivial problem requiring learning strategies which are still very much the subject of research.

Let us look at a few examples of second-generation expert systems.

Example 1

NEOMYCIN (Clancey and Letsinger, 1981) is one of the first examples of a second-generation expert system. It uses the technique of meta-rules to implement problem solving knowledge. For example, the differential diagnosis strategy is represented in the rule contained in Fig. 6. The strategy rules make use of domain theories such as a taxonomy of diseases (cf. Fig. 3), models of disease processes, causal networks, etc.

META-RULE 397 (for the task Group-and-Differentiate)

IF: There are two items on the differential that differ in some disease process feature
THEN: Ask a question that differentiates between these two kinds of processes.

Fig. 6 — Explicit problem solving strategy in NEOMYCIN.

NEOMYCIN did not have a component representing the heuristic rules themselves. It would always carry out its reasoning based on the explicitly represented strategies. This is a reasonable approach when the strategic knowledge maps straightforwardly to problem solutions. However, if various strategies are tried or if a strategy involves many reasoning steps that can be left out in the resulting rule, it is more appropriate also explicitly to store the resulting rule for later use.

Example 2

The LEX system (Mitchell *et al.*, 1984) is interesting not so much by the breadth of its expertise, but because it was one of the first second-generation expert systems capable of generating shallow knowledge by exercising the deep knowledge and then extracting a heuristic rule using machine learning techniques. Deep knowledge is in the form of operators for symbolic integration, such as contained in Fig. 7.

Blind application of these operators generates a search space which is explored using weak methods. However, once a search path had been found leading from a problem to a solution, an attempt is made to extract heuristic

OP1: $\int r \cdot f(x)\, dx \Rightarrow r \int f(x)\, dx$
OP2: $\int u\, dv \Rightarrow uv - \int v\, du$
. . .

Fig. 7 — The domain theory of LEX.

rules to capture the experience. An example of such a rule is contained in Fig. 8.

Note that the LEX program does not have an explicit representation of the strategic knowledge underlying the formation of rules. This knowledge is implicit in the learning algorithm.

Other second-generation expert systems have since been built that follow the same schema. For example, at the VUB AI laboratory a prototype second-generation expert system for causal diagnosis of technical systems has been constructed (Steels and Van de Velde, 1986). It starts from domain theories in the form of causal networks. When there are no heuristic rules covering the situation, it falls back on weak problem-solving methods. Afterwards rules are extracted by a learning method called progressive refinement.

Example 3
XPLAIN (Swartout, 1981) is another early example motivated by better explanation facilities. It has an explicit representation of domain theories in the form of causal models containing facts such as 'increased digitalis can cause a change to ventricular fibrillation'. An example of the problem-solving knowledge is contained in Fig. 9. Swartout's strategies are usually more domain-oriented than the ones used in NEOMYCIN.

Swartout used an original method to combine domain theories and problem-solving knowledge into shallow knowledge, namely automatic programming. Heuristic rules are compiled analytically by specializing problem-solving strategies to the domain theory. This is different from the mechanisms used by Mitchell *et al.* which learn shallow knowledge within the context of particular experiences. An important aspect of XPLAIN is that the genesis of a specific rule is available to the system for providing better explanations.

The examples given here are not intended to be an exhaustive survey. They illustrate, however, the basic idea: there is an explicit representation of deep knowledge in the form of domain theories and problem-solving knowledge. Reasoning is either done directly using deep knowledge (as in NEOMYCIN) or with heuristic rules which are generated out of the deep knowledge (as in XPLAIN).

The advantages of a second-generation architecture are numerous:
(1) The expert system is closer to a model of the human expert which also utilizes deep knowledge, particularly when he does not yet have heuristic rules available.
(2) There is a graceful performance degradation. When there are no heuristic rules available to solve the problem quickly, the system can fall

IF: The expression is of the form ∫ x transc(x) d(x)
THEN: Use Operator2 (integration by parts)
        with u = x
        and dv = transc(x) dx

Fig. 8 — Heuristic rule in LEX.

Goal: Anticipate Drug Toxicity
Domain Rationale:
       Presence of finding causes dangerous deviation
       Increased drug causes dangerous deviation
Problem Solving Method:
 IF the Finding exists
 THEN reduce the drug dose
 ELSE maintain the drug dose.

Fig. 9 — Problem solving strategy in XPLAIN.

back on deeper knowledge and try to find a solution using weaker methods.

(3) There are better explanations. Instead of simply returning the heuristic rules that were used to solve the problem, the system can explain the rationale behind a rule.

(4) There is the potential for automatic knowledge acquisition as illustrated by LEX and other learning expert systems.

8.   CONCLUSIONS

The chapter has reviewed the current trend towards deeper expert systems that counteracts the tendency towards trivialization and superficiality. Deeper expert systems have two kinds of knowledge:

(1) Deep knowledge which consists of domain theories and problem solving knowledge.

(2) Shallow knowledge which is similar to the heuristic rules found in first-generation expert systems.

The chapter discusses a few systems with these characteristics and argues why they constitute progress towards more solid expert systems.

REFERENCES

Bennett, J. S. (1983) ROGET: a knowledge-based consultant for acquiring the conceptual structure of an expert system. *Memo HPP-83-24*, Stanford University, Department of Computer Science.

Breuker, J. and Wielinga, B. (1985) KADS: structured knowledge acquisition for expert systems. *5th International Workshop on Expert Systems and their Applications*, Agence de L'Informatique, Avignon, pp. 887–900.

Buchanan, B. and Mitchell, T. (1978) Model-directed learning of production rules. In D. Waterman and R. Hayes-Roth (eds.)

Clancey, W. J. (1979) Transfer of rule-based expertise through a tutoring dialogue. *Ph.D. Dissertation*, Stanford University.

Clancey, W. J. (1982) The epistemology of rule-based expert systems: a framework for explanation. *AI Journal* **20**(3) 215–251.

Clancey, W. J. (1985) Heuristic classification. *AI Journal* **27**(4) 289–350.

Clancey, W. J. and Letsinger, R. (1981) NEOMYCIN: reconfiguring a rule-based expert system for application to teaching. *Proceedings of the 7th IJCAI, Vancouver, B.C., Canada*, pp. 829–836.

Davis, R. (1982) Expert systems: where are we? And where do we go from here? *MIT AI Lab. Memo 665.*

De Wael, L. (1987) Steps towards a methodology for expert system development. *IEEE Transactions on Simulation Journal A* **28**(1).

Feigenbaum, E. A., Buchanan, B. G. and Lederberg, J. (1971) On generality and problem solving: a case study using the DENDRAL program. *Machine Intelligence*, American Elsevier, New York, pp. 165–190.

Hobbs, J. R. and Moore, R. C. (1985) *Formal Theories of the Commonsense World*, Ablex, Norwood, New Jersey.

Lenat, D. (1983) The role of heuristics in learning by discovery: three case studies. In: Michalski *et al.* (1984), pp. 243–306.

McDermott, J. (1980) R1: a rule-based configurer of computer systems. *Technical Report*, Carnegie–Mellon University, Department of Computer Science.

Michalski, R. S. (1983) A theory and methodology of inductive learning. *AI Journal* **20**(2) 111–161.

Michalski, R., Carbonell, J., and Mitchell, T. (eds.) (1984) *Machine Learning. An Artificial Intelligence Approach*, Springer Verlag, Berlin.

Mitchell, T. M. (1978) Version spaces: an approach to concept learning. *Ph.D. Dissertation*, Stanford University.

Mitchell, T. M., Utgoff, P., and Banerji, R. (1984) Learning by experimentation: acquiring and refining problem-solving heuristics. In: Michalski *et al.* (1984), pp. 163–190.

Shortliffe, E. H. (1976) MYCIN: a rule-based computer program for advising physicians regarding antimicrobial therapy selection. *Ph.D. Dissertation*, Stanford University.

Smith, R. (1984) On the development of commercial expert systems. *AI Magazine* (Fall 1984) pp. 61–73.

Steels, L. (1984) Second generation expert systems. *Conference on Future Generation Computer Systems, Rotterdam.* In: *Journal of Future Generation Computer Systems*, **1** (4 June 1985).

Steels, L. and Van de Velde, W. (1986) Learning in second generation expert systems. In: Kowalik (ed.) *Knowledge- based Problem Solving*, Prentice-Hall, Englewood Ciffs, New Jersey, pp. 270–295.

Swartout, W. (1981) Producing explanations and justifications of expert consulting programs. *Ph.D. Dissertation,* Massachusetts Institute of Technology.

Wielinga, B. J. and Breuker, J. A. (1984) Interpretation of verbal data for knowledge acquisition. *Proceedings of ECAI 84,* North-Holland, Amsterdam, pp. 41–50.

2

Contribution of hybrid and hierarchical representation of knowledge to the explanation of reasoning

B. Causse, A. Hocine, H. Touhami
Laboratoire d'Informatique, Faculté des Sciences et
Techniques, Avenue des l'Université, 64000 Pau, France

SUMMARY

This chapter deals with a methodology for explaining the reasoning (including the classical trace) of expert systems based on a hybrid (production rules and frames) and hierarchical representation of the knowledge, making it better structured so that a more precise explanation can be obtained from entity production rules and frames.

1. INTRODUCTION

Expert systems should be able to provide, to explain, and to justify their reasoning.

The explanation modules of most expert systems based on production rules merely give the trace, i.e. the list of rules that have been used during the reasoning process. This type of system's explanation rests upon the list of rules arising in the resolution of the problem, using the logical deduction of the expert system.

This approach has certain failings:

— There is only one form of knowledge representation. Production rules only represent knowledge that allows the making of inferences: no account is taken of the field of knowledge, while each field needs specific adaptations (Assemat and Bonnett 1986).
— The presentation of an explanation in the form of a succession of rules is not sufficiently concise.
— In the results produced, the information necessary to determine the origin of an action is mixed with small points that hide what is essential.

In order to make up for some of these failings, we recommend a method of explanation in an expert system based on a hybrid representation of knowledge (Hocine and Touhami, 1986) using two complementary forms of representation: production rules and frames derived from the notion of the 'frame' defined originally by Minsky.

The general architecture of this expert system is the following:

(a) a knowledge base of the field of application made up of
      — production rules divided by the expert into groups
      — meta-rules which are knowledge of the rules and the groups of rules
(b) a multi-criterion inference engine made up of
      — an inference mechanism
      — a knowledge of the control strategy described by frames
(c) a 'facts base'.

2. THE REPRESENTATION OF KNOWLEDGE

Two kinds of knowledge are dealt with:

(a) Static knowledge, corresponding to the aims of the field and the current situation described by the user. This includes:
      — simple facts corresponding to independent aims
      — structured facts described by frames
(b) Dynamic knowledge, which allows
      — the definition of relations between the aims of the static knowledge
      — reasoning about itself (on the level of meta-knowledge)
      This meta-knowledge is made up of:
      — production rules operating on the static knowledge and/or the rules themselves (meta-rules)
      — frames describing the control structure

The use of this hybrid represenation has required the development of software to representation and manipulation of 'frames', allowing the use of the notion of hierarchy and inheritance.

2.1 Production rules
The production rules that express the knowledge of the field are expressed in the usual form

$$IF < conditions > THEN < actions >$$

An example of a rule is

> If   position leaf = base of stem
> and   appearance leaf = hairy
> and   arrangement leaf = bow
> and   shape leaf = ellipital
> Then name family leaf = primulaceae

Each entity (leaf, stem, environment, flower, ...) used in a rule has a frame associated with it.

2.2   Frames

A frame is a data structure that describes a prototypical situation by the use of a group of characteristics. It is an effective and certain method of forgetting nothing when a concept is dealt with.

A frame is defined by a name and a list of attributes; each attribute is described by a list of predefined facets and the values that are associated with it.

The general form of a frame is the following:

```
(name-frame
(attribute1   (facet1 value1 ... valuen)
              (facet2 value1 ... valuen)
              (facetn value1 ... valuen)
)
(attribute1   (facet1 value1 ... valuen)
              (facet2 value1 ... valuen)
              (facetn value1 ... valuen)
)
)
```

The software tool developed for representing and manipulating this knowledge with the help of frames has several predefined facets (the identifiers of these facets always begin with the character $).

The attributes are chosen by the user. It is to be noted that there are some predefined attributes that have a link is-a (est-un) which allows an example to inherit frames directly that are hierarchically superior to it.

The totality of these facets defines the semantics of the representation. They make it possible to define completely an attribute by its type ($un, $listede), the associated value ($valeur) or by default ($defaut), the restrictions ($domaine, $intervalle), the means of obtaining a value ($si-besoin), the unit of measure ($unité), the detailed description ($description), a rational explanation ($explication) and so on.

The basic types that are predefined are text (texte), real (réel), integer (entier), boolean (booléen) and symbol (symbole).

Some examples of entity frames

The family frame is:

```
(frame-family
    (fam-name     ($un texte))
    (stem         ($un frame-stem))
    (flower       ($un frame-flower))
    (leaf         ($un frame-leaf))
    (environment ($un frame-environment))
)
```

An instance of this frame is:

```
(primulaceae
```

```
        (est-un          ($valeur frame-family))
        (fam-name        ($valeur primulaceae))
        (stem            ($valeur stem-pr))
        (flower          ($valeur flower-pr))
        (leaf            ($un leaf-pr))
        (environment ($valeur environment-pr))
    )
```

stem-pr, flower-pr, leaf-pr and environment-pr are particular cases of the frames frame-stem, frame-flower, frame-leaf and frame-environment.

The frame frame-stem is:

```
(frame-stem
        (form ($un texte)
                ($domaine "round" "square" "triangular"
                "rectangular")
                ($defaut "round")
                ($description "form of the stem")
        )
        (appearance ($un texte)
                ($domaine "rarely hairy" "hairy" "woody"
                "herbaceous")
                ($description "consistency of the stem")
                ($explication "can only be round, square, triangu-
                lar or rectangular")
        )
        (colour  ($un frame-colour-stem))
        (habit   ($un texte)
                ($domaine "erect" "creeping" "climbing")
        )
    )
```

The frame frame-colour is:

```
(frame-colour-stem
        (colour ($valeur green)
                ($description "the colour of the stem")
                ($explication "can only be one colour")
                )
    )
```

An instance of the frame frame-stem is:

```
(stem-primulaceae
        (est-un          ($valeur frame-stem))
        (form            ($valeur "round"))
        (appearance      ($valeur herbaceous))
        (colour          ($valeur colour-2))
        (habit           ($valeur erect))
    )
```

An instance of the frame frame-colour-stem is:

```
(colour-2
        (colour ($valeur green))
)
```

The use of the two following facets is particularly to be noted:

— $description
— $explication

The examples used to illustrate our approach are taken from an application on the flora of the Pyrenees currently being developed. The objective of this application is to be able to identify a plant. The process of identification is based upon the recognition of characteristics possessed by each family.

The description of different features is done by visual observation, by touch and finally by odour at the level of the species.

A second phase will consist of the determination of the genus and the species of each plant.

2.3   The facets: $description and $explication

The facet $description

This allows us to provide the exact title of the attribute. The user might not know the significance of terms used by the system beforehand; the meaning of the term is thus shown at the time of the explanation.

Example:

plant type = primulaceae

will be translated into:

The family of this plant is of the primulaceae type:

Thanks to this facet there is no need to write a sentence generator, but merely to access the frame of the entity and to reproduce the value associated with the $description facet.

The facet $explication

This facet is activated when the user asks for an explanation of the type *why*. It allows, first of all, the rational explanation of the expert to be provided.

To improve the explanation, it is necessary to know the origin (or the source) of the values assigned to the attributes. Let us demonstrate this necessity through the example below.

Consider the following frame:

```
(person
        (name           ($un texte))
        (address        ($un texte))
        (no-days-work    ($un entier)
                        ($defaut 5)
```

                    ($description "Number of working days per
                    week"))
      (no-hours-work ($description "Number of working hours per
                    week')
                    ($si-besoin-demander
                        (print "give the number of hours of
                        work")
                        (sput-v frame-no-hours-work(read)))
                    ($si-besoin-calculer
                        (sput-v sch no-hours-work(no-days-work
                        8))
                    ($default 16))
)

Consider the following instance of the frame person:

    (person1
        (name   ($valeur "henry IV"))
        (address   ($valeur "rue serviez PAU"))
        (no-days-work ($valeur 2))
        (no-hours-work ($valeur 16))
)

In this instance, the value (16) associated with the attribute no-hours-work is brought about by the facet $valeur but absolutely nothing can be said concerning the origin of this value, i.e.

— was it calculated?
— was it read (i.e. asked for)?
— was it obtained by default?

The content of any fact can only be explained if the way in which it was obtained is known.

One of the extensions of this system in relation to others, of which FRL is one, is to cover up this failing. Indeed, at the level of implementation, the facet that produced the value of each attribute of a frame is shown; this is particularly realized in the explanation phase.

3.   THE EXPLANATION MODULE

3.1   Presentation and working

The aim of this approach is to provide the user with a clear explanation that interprets the behaviour of the expert system when it makes its deductions.

The idea consists, in a first step, of explaining the reasoning from the starting point of the rules, then of making this explanation complete using information contained in the frames. To do this, the explanation module records the origin of each fact's deduction during reasoning in order to be able to reproduce the tree diagram of the deduction at the end (this is the usual trace). Simultaneously, it organizes the facts base, putting together all the facts concerning the same entities (plant, flower, type, ...) (Kassel, 1986). A first form of explanation is thus provided, starting from the diagram deduction tree and the contents of the facts base.

3.2   The types of questions that could be asked

We are interested in two types of question:

— How was a fact deduced?
— Why did a predicate applied to a certain entity take a certain value?

Examples:

— How was fam-name plant = primulaceae deduced?
— Why does size plant = 20?

To reply to a question of the type how, we must explain the behaviour of the system. In fact, we make use of the tree diagram of deduction and the contents of the facts base by giving the rules that have led to the deduction of a fact; this is not sufficient to justify reasoning. It is at this level that we use the tree diagram of frames.

The facts base is structured in such a way as to allow the grouping, during reasoning, of all the facts relating to an entity.

In the following example, 'leaf' is the entity concerned in the reasoning:

If   position leaf = base-of-stem
and appearance leaf = hairy
and arrangement leaf = bow
and shape leaf = ellipitical
Then family name of leaf = primulaceae

Following the triggering of this rule, we find the following group of facts concerning the entity leaf in the facts base:

position leaf = base-of-stem
appearance leaf = hairy
arrangement leaf = bow
shape leaf = elliptical
family-name leaf = primulaceae

This structuring allows all that has been deduced about a given entity to be found easily when an explanation has been generated in order to reply to a question of the type how.

3.3   The generation of explanations from rules and frames

The representation of knowledge used allows us two levels of explanation (how and why):

— The first is based on the use of the tree diagram of deduction and on the way in which the values are obtained in order to divide the tree of deduction into groups, each one corresponding to a part of the reasoning and to an entity.
— The second allows the making of an explanation from the entity frames

through the facets $description and $explication. The path of the tree of deduction is not fixed in advance; it depends entirely on the user's answers.

Example:

The reply to the question

HOW DID YOU DEDUCE fam-name plant = primulaceae?

The system prints:

WE HAVE COME TO THIS CONCLUSION BY:
      fam-name stem = primulaceae
      fam-name flower = primulaceae
      fam-leaf = primulaceae
      size plant = 20
      appearance plant = herbaceous

All this information is taken from the group of rules concerning the entity plant, containing in this case just one rule:

    If   fam-name stem = primulaceae
    and fam-name flower = primulaceae
    and fam-name leaf = primulaceae
    and size plant = 20
    and appearance plant = herbaceous
    Then fam-name plant = primulaceae

If the user does not understand the meaning of the terms used by the system, a clearer explanation is provided by the facets $description and $explication.

Thus we would have:

WE HAVE COME TO THIS CONCLUSION BY:
   — the family of the stem of the plant is primulaceae
   — the family of the leaf of the plant is primulaceae
   — the family of the flower of the plant is primulaceae
   — the size of the plant is equal to 20 cm
   — the appearance of the plant is hairy

In this explanation, the presence of two types of information should be noted:

   — a first type concerning the stem, the leaf and the flower
   — a second type concerning the plant (size, environment, odour)

Let us suppose for instance that user is not convinced that:

   the stem of the plant is of the primulaceae family.

Since (fam-name type = pr) is a fact that can be deduced, a first explanation will be given by the rules. We therefore once again make use of the tree diagram and more exactly of the group of rules concerning 'stem' to produce a new explanation.

In the reverse case, where the question concerns 'plant' for example:

WHY size plant = 20?

the explanation given by the rules is no longer sufficient and we thus use the knowledge structured through entity frames.

We note that the path through the tree diagram of deduction or the frame tree diagram is not fixed in advance; it will depend entirely on the answer of the user.

To reply to the question:

WHY size plant = 20?

the entity frame plant allows the production, by means of its facet $explication, of:

Primulaceae plants are very small

If this explanation is convincing, we stop the explanation process; otherwise, we show the range of values taken by size, followed by the unit:

(frame-name plant = pr) ← (size plant = 20) ← frame size

Example of a message:
— size ≤ 20 cm and size ≥ 10 cm

The range values and the unit of measure are taken from the frame plant.

There are several situations where the expression of an explanation by means of synthesis is not enough (the case of an arithmetic expression). We have thus provided for the printing of the formula of calculation that was used in our module (see the facet $si-besoin-calculer) and we define all the variables used in a formula by giving the value taken by each one.

In this application for flora, another method of explanation is being considered: the use of graphs. A possible explanation would be to draw a picture of the flower showing its form, colour and appearance.

4.   CONCLUSION

This approach to explanation by the use of production rules and frames structured hierarchically has allowed us to obtain a much more satisfactory explanation and justification than with the usual trace.

In the application for the determination of flora we started by simply dealing with families; the determination of the type and species will complete this system and may well bring up other problems.

REFERENCES

Assemat, C. and Bonnet, A. (1986) Conceptualisation, cohérence et validation des bases de connaissances. *Congrés les systèmes experts et leur application, Avignon, juin 1986*, pp. 299–319.

Bensaid, A., Rechenmann, F., Simonet, A., and Vignard, P. (1986) Mécanismes d'inférences et d'explication dans les bases de connaissances centrées objet. *8émes journées francophones sur l'informatique, Grenoble, janvier 1986*, pp. 15–27.

Hocine, A. and Touhami, H. (1986) Un système expert pour l'application des textes d'une réglementation énorme et/ou complexe. *1ère Conférence internationale l'économique et l'intelligence artificielle, septembre 1986*, pp. 125–130.

Kassel, G. (1986) Expliquer c'est raisonner sur le raisonnement le système CQFE. *Congrés les systèmes experts et leur application, Avignon, juin 1986*, pp. 973–990.

Lauriere, J. L. (1982) Représentation et utilisation des connaissances. *Revue TSI n° 1 et 2*, Dunod.

Safar, B. (1985) Les explications dans les systèmes experts. *Cognitiva 85*, pp. 459–464.

Swartout, W. R. (1983) XPLAIN: a system for creating and explaining consulting program. *Artificial Intelligence* (21) 285–325.

Winston, P. H. and Horn, B. K. P. (1984) *LISP*, Addison-Wesley.

3

Analogous dissimilarities

Christel Vrain and **Yves Kodratoff**
Equipe Inférence et Apprentissage, Bat. 490, Laboratoire de Recherche en Informatique, UA 410 CNRS, Université de Paris Sud, 91405 Orsay Cédex, France

SUMMARY

Analogy is clearly one of the key issues of learning. This chapter presents our view of analogy: we must take into account not only the resemblances within a set of data but also the differences between them. We propose a simple application of the analogical process to incremental learning.

1. INTRODUCTION

From the point of view of the stategies that are used, one tends now to put machine learning under several headings: constructive learning which includes the EBL (Mitchell *et al.*, 1986) and EBG (DeJong and Mooney, 1986) systems, inductive learning, as developed in the system INDUCE (Michalski, 1983), analogy (Carbonell, 1982), etc.

In this chapter, we give our point of view about analogy and show with a simple example how we could use its techniques in the domain of concept formation from a set of examples.

1.1 Causal reasoning

Analogy theory relies on causal reasoning. This kind of reasoning may use three different forms of inference:

— The classical formal inference.
— The uncertain or possible inference.
— The 'causal' inference where we only suggest that a fact is linked to some causes. For instance, when we say that the climate of a town is linked to its geographical position and to its latitude, we only express a relation of causality.

We shall not go into further details on causal reasoning in this paper.

1.2 Classical analogy

In this paper, we start from the classical paradigm of analogy (Chouraqui, 1985):

A′ is analogous to B′ in the same way as A is analogous to B

which can be illustrated by the diagram shown in Fig. 1.

The phore {A, B} is the information that bears the analogy. It therefore describes the situation from which one starts. Between A and B, there is a causality relation, called c(A, B), which enables one to infer B from A.

The theme {A′, B′} is the result of the analogy; it contains the information that has been completed by analogy.

Between A and A′ (respectively between B and B′), there is a similarity relation, written s(A A′) (respectively written s′(B, B′)).

Between A′ and B′, there is a causality relation, written c′(A′, B′).

Example: For instance, let us suppose that we apply techniques of analogy to translate sentences from French to English.

We may have A = une bicyclette rouge, which can be described by:

> (composed-by une bicyclette rouge) & (article une) & (indefinite une) & (noun bicyclette) & (feminine bicylette) & (singular bicylette) & (adjective rouge)

This conjunction expresses the fact that the sentence is composed of *at least* three words: 'une', 'bicylette' and 'rouge', that the word 'une' is an indefinite article, that the word 'bicyclette' is a feminine and singular noun and that the word 'rouge' is an adjective.

A′ = des bicylettes rouges can be described by:

> (composed-by des bicyclettes rouges) & (article des) & (indefinite des) &
> (noun bicyclettes) & (feminine bicyclettes) & (plural bicyclettes bicyclette) &
> (adjective rouges) & (rout rouges rouge)

The expression '(root bicyclettes bicyclette)' indicates that the word 'bicyclettes' comes from the noun 'bicyclette'.

B = a red bike can be be described by the conjunction:

> (composed-by a red bike) & (article a) & (indefinite a) &
> (noun bike) & (neuter bike) & (singular bike) &
> (adjective red)

B′ = red bikes can be described by:

> (composed-by red bikes) & (noun bikes) & (neuter bikes) &
> (plural bikes) & (root bikes bike) & (adjective red)

We can compute the similarity between A and A′:

> s(A, A′) = (composed-by x y z) & (article x) & (indefinite x) &
> (noun y) & (feminine y) & (adjective z)

It expresses the fact that the sentence is made of three words, i.e. x, y and z, that x is an indefinite article, y is a feminine noun and z is an adjective.

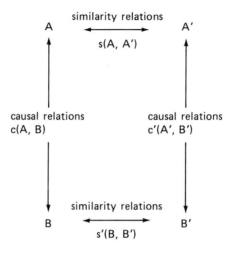

Fig. 1.

We can also compute the similarity between B and B':

$$s'(B, B') = \text{(composed-by x y) \& (adjective x) \& (noun y) \& (neuter y)}$$

We can define the following causality relations between A and B, $c(A, B)$:

c_1: "in English, 'a' is an indefinite article"

c_2: "in English, an adjective, used as an attribute is placed before the noun"

c_3: "in English, an adjective is invariable"

c_4: "the word 'red' is the translation of the word 'rouge' "

c_5: "the word 'bike' is the translation of the word 'bicyclette' "

The set of causality relations between A' and B', $c'(A', B')$, is composed of c^2, c^3, c^4, c^5 and of:

c^6: "in English, there are no plural and indefinite articles"

c^7: "the plural noun 'bikes' is obtained by adding an 's' to the translation of the word 'bicyclette' "

Referring to the general scheme, if we know A, B, $c(A, B)$ and A' and if we are able to compute the similarities $s(A, A')$ between A and A', then we know causality relations between A' and B', and can therefore deduce similarities between B and B' and partially infer B'.

Example: In our example, let us suppose that we only know A, B, $c(A, B)$ and A'. We can easily compute $s(A, A')$: the two expressions A and A' have three common features: an indefinite article, a feminine noun and an adjective. We are interested in the causality relations between A and B, the preconditions of which contain some of these common features. In our example, this last condition is satisfied by all the causality relations c^1, c^2, c^3, c^4 and c^5. We can apply these relations to A' and we may infer for B' that we may use the indefinite article 'a', that the adjective 'red' is placed before the noun 'bike'. It is not sufficient to translate A' correctly.

If we take into account the dissimilarities between A and B, we notice that the expression A is a singular one whereas the expression B is a plural one. We can verify whether the causality relations that use common features do not use discriminate features and we can also search for new causality relations, based on these discriminant features. In our example, the causality relation c^1 is correct only for a singular expression and we need the causality relations, c^6 and c^7 to infer B' correctly.

2.   ANALOGIES AND DISSIMILARITIES

We have shown the importance of the dissimilarities in the analogy process.

We still suppose that we have a phore $\{A, B\}$ and a theme $\{A', B'\}$ but now we also take into account the dissimilarities between A and A' and between B and B'.

Let us denote by $\mathrm{sd}(A, A') = [s_A \mid d_A \leftarrow d_{A'}]$ the similarity and dissimilarity relations between A and A'. Here, s_A represents the similarities between A and A' and $d_A \leftarrow d_{A'}$ means that d is an element of A and that it must be replaced by d' to obtain the corresponding element of A'; it therefore represents the dissimilarities between A and A' (see Fig. 2).

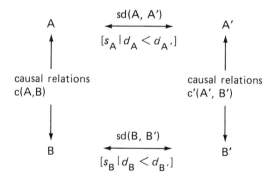

Fig. 2.

Let $\mathrm{sd}(A, A')$ be the similarity and dissimilarity relation between A and A'. It is given by:

$$\mathrm{sd}(A, A') = [s_A \mid d_A \leftarrow d_{A'}]$$

Let sd(B, B') be the similarity and dissimilarity relation between B and B'. It is given by:

$$sd(B, B') = [S_B \mid d_B \leftarrow d_{B'}]$$

Example: Let us consider again the example of Section 1.2.

We can compute the similarity and dissimilarity relation between A and A':

$$sd(A, A') = [(\text{composed-by x y z}) \& (\text{article x}) \& (\text{indefinite x}) \&$$
$$(\text{noun y}) \& (\text{feminine y}) \& (\text{adjective z}) \mid (\text{singular y})$$
$$\leftarrow (\text{plural y})]$$

It expresses the fact that the two expressions A and A' are made of three words, i.e. x, y and z, x being an indefinite article, y being a feminine noun and z being an adjective, but in A the noun y is singular and in A' it is a plural.

We can also compute the similarity and dissimilarity relation between B and B':

$$sd'(B, B') = [(\text{composed-by x y}) \& (\text{adjective x}) \&$$
$$(\text{noun y}) \& (\text{neuter y}) \mid (\text{singular y}) \leftarrow (\text{plural y})]$$

The causality relations between A and B and between A' and B' are the same as in Section 1.2.

Suppose that one is able to find the following causality relations:

R1 between s_A and s_B,
R2 between d_A and d_B,
R3 between $d_{A'}$ and $d_{B'}$

We suggest the following analogy paradigm:

Knowing A, B, A', s_A, d_A and $d_{A'}$ and being able to compute R1, R2 and R3 from some general knowledge, one is then able to infer s_B, d_B and $d_{B'}$, and therefore to invent B', which is a new concept or a new rule, learned by anology.

Example: In our previous example, suppose that we know A, B, A', sd(A, B) and the causality relations c^1, c^2, c^3, c^4, c^5, c^6 and c^7 and that we want to find the English translation of the expression B. We recall that:

A = une bicyclette rouge
B = a red bike
A' = des bicyclettes rouge
$$sd(A, A') = = [(\text{composed-by x y z}) \& (\text{article x}) \& (\text{indefinite x})$$
$$\&$$
$$(\text{noun y}) \& (\text{feminine y}) \& (\text{adjective z}) \mid (\text{singular}$$
$$\text{y}) \leftarrow (\text{plural y})]$$

We have two causality relations based on the notion of indefinite article: c^1 and c^6. To choose among them, we can notice that in the second one, c^6, we have the notion of 'plural and indefinite article' and the property 'plural' is a difference between A and A'. We may wonder whether c^1 is still true for a plural and indefinite article. The article 'a' is not a plural and indefinite article. Therefore, we can only apply c^6. We can use the other causality relations between A and B. We can also apply the causality relation c^7 based on the notion of 'plural'. We can now infer the correct expression of B':

$$B' = \text{red bikes}$$

To take into account the differences between A and B is not always sufficient to infer B' correctly, but it leads to a better result than using only the resemblances between A and B.

Our definition contains the classical one which is restricted to the analogy between s_A and s_B. It also defines an analogy between the dissimilarities $[d_A \leftarrow d_{A'}]$ and $[d_B \leftarrow d_{B'}]$.

3. A SIMPLE APPLICATION TO INCREMENTAL LEARNING OF CONCEPTS

Let us suppose that we have p examples $E^1, \ldots, E_p$ of the same concept C and let us suppose that these examples are described by n attributes $A_1, \ldots, A_n$:

$$E_i = [A_1 = val_1^i] \& \ldots \& [A_n = val_n^i]$$

An attribute may be nominal (the possible values of this attribute are independent), linear (the possible values are ordered) or structured (the possible values are leaves of a given taxonomy) (Michalski, 1983).

Example: For instance, we may have the following descriptions of persons:

$$E_1 = [\text{kind} = \text{boy}] \& [\text{age} = 13] \& [\text{colour-eyes} = \text{blue}]$$
$$E_2 = [\text{kind} = \text{girl}] \& [\text{age} = 15] \& [\text{colour-eyes} = \text{brown}]$$

The descriptor 'kind' is a structured one. Its values are leaves of the taxonomy tax_1 (see Fig. 3).

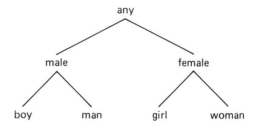

Fig. 3.

The descriptor 'age' is a linear one. Its values are integers, ranging from 0 to 100. The descriptor 'colour-eyes' is a nominal one. Its possible values are 'blue', 'green', 'brown', 'grey'.

A generalization G of these examples is described by the conjunction:

$$G = [A_1 = val_1^G] \& \ldots \& [A_n = val_n^G]$$

where the value val_i^G of the attribute A_i is defined as follows:

(i) If the descriptor A_i is nominal, $val_i^G = val_i^1 \vee \ldots \vee val_i^p$, where for $j = 1, \ldots, p$, val_i^j is the value of the descriptor A_i in the example E_j.

(ii) If the descriptor A_i is linear, $val_i^G = val_i^l \ldots val_i^m$, which means that A_i may take all the values ranging from val_i^l to val_i^m. The integers l and m are specified by:

$$\forall j \in \{1, \ldots, n\} \, val_i^l \leqslant valsubi_i^j \leqslant val_i^m.$$

(iii) If the descriptor A_i is structured, val_i^G is the least common ancestor of $val_i^1, \ldots, val_i^p$.

Example: A generalization of our two previous examples is:

$$G = [\text{kind} = \text{any}] \& [\text{age} = 13 \ldots 15] \&$$
$$[\text{colour-eyes} = \text{blue} \vee \text{brown}]$$

Suppose now that we learn a new example, called E_{p+1} of the concept C. We have to see whether G is also a generalization of E_{p+1}, and, if it is not satisfied, we have to modify G to cover this new example.

We know the causal relations between an example E_i, $i = 1, \ldots, p$, and the generalization G — they are given by definitions (i), (ii) and (iii) — and therefore we can use reasoning by analogy to find a new generalization G' of $E_1, \ldots, E_p, E_{p+1}$. The anological process can be illustrated by the diagram shown in Fig. 4.

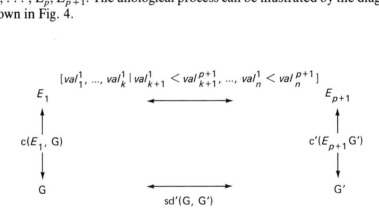

Fig. 4.

For the sake of simplicity, we suppose that we compare E_{p+1} with E_1 and that the values of the k attributes $A_1, \ldots, A_k$ are the same for E_1 and E_{p+1}.

For all the integers j, $(j = 1, \ldots, k)$, $val_j^1 = val_j^{p+1}$ and val_j^k is a generalization of the different values $val_j^1, \ldots, val_j^p$. The value val_j^G is therefore a generalization of $val_j^1, \ldots, val_j^p, val_j^{p+1}$ and

$$val_j^{G'} = val_j^G.$$

Let j be an integer, belonging to $\{k + 1, \ldots, n\}$. To find the value of $val_j^{G'}$, we have to generalise val_j^G and val_j^{p+1}.

Example: Suppose now that we have a new example E_3 of the concept illustrated by E_1 and E_2:

$$E_3 = [\text{kind} = \text{boy}] \,\&\, [\text{age} = 17] \,\&\, [\text{colour-eyes} = \text{blue}]$$

The example E_3 is not an instance of the generalization G of E_1 and E_2:

$$G = [\text{kind} = \text{any}] \,\&\, [\text{age} = 13 \ldots 15] \,\&$$
$$[\text{colour-eyes} = \text{brown} \lor \text{brown}].$$

We have to find a new description G′ which generalises E_1, E_2 and E_3. In order to find G′, let us find analogies between E_1 and E_3. We obtain the analogies shown in Fig. 5.

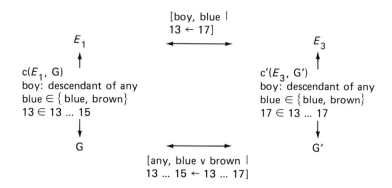

Fig. 5.

The examples E_1 and E_3 have the same values for the descriptors 'kind' and 'colour-eyes'. The value of the descriptor 'age' in G must be generalized to cover the value '17'. We obtain

$$G' = [\text{kind} = \text{any}] \,\&\, [\text{age} = 13 \ldots 17] \,\&$$
$$[\text{colour-eyes} = \text{blue} \lor \text{brown}]$$

This process is efficient only if we can find good analogies between E_1 and E_{p+1}. We have to choose the example E_j, $j \in \{1, \ldots, p\}$, which is the most similar to E_{p+1}. We have therefore to define a notion of similarity between two examples E_j and E_{p+1}. It could be:

— the number of attributes the values of which are the same for E_k and E_{p+1}, or
— for each other attribute A_i, the distance between the two different values val_i^j and val_i^{p+1} or their degree of generality if the attribute is structured.

We can also give more importance to some attributes than to others.

The use of analogy seems perhaps trivial in this kind of representation of the examples and of the generalization G. However, let us suppose now that the generalization G may also be made of derived descriptors, which are found by applying theorems to the examples.

Example: For instance, suppose that in our previous example, we know also the following theorems:

R_1: [age < 12] & [kind = boy ∨ girl]   ⇒ [period-life = childhood]
R_2: [age = 12 . . . 18] & [kind = boy ∨ girl] ⇒ [period-life = adolescence]
R_3: [age > 18]   ⇒ [kind = man ∨ woman]
R_4: [kind = man ∨ woman]   ⇒ [period-life ∨ adult]

A better generalization of E_1 and E_2 is therefore:

$$G_1 = [\text{kind = any}] \& [\text{age = 13 . . . 15}] \&$$
$$[\text{colour-eyes = blue} \vee \text{brown}] \&$$
$$[\text{period-life = adolescence}]$$

Suppose that the generalization G of the examples $E_1, \ldots, E_p$ contains new derived descriptors $[A_d = val_d^G]$ and suppose that we have to modify G to cover the new example E_{p+1}.

We know that there are theorems which may be applied to E_1 to prove that it satisfies the descriptor $[A_d = val_d^G]$. We try to apply these theorems to E_{p+1}. If this is not possible, we have to prove that E_{p+1} satisfies also the descriptor $[A_d = val_d^G]$.

Example: G_1 does not cover the example E_3. In order to improve it and to find a generalization of E_1 E_2 and E_3, let us find analogies between E_1 and E_3. We obtain the analogies shown in Fig. 6.

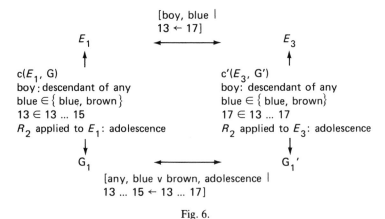

Fig. 6.

To find the value of the descriptor 'period-life' in the generalization G_1', we try to apply the theorem R_2 which was applied to E_1 and E_3. It succeeds. If it had failed, we would have had to prove, if possible, that E_3 was also in the period of life of adolescence. Nevertheless, the proof that E_1 satisfies the property [period-life = adolescence] may guide us.

In the example, the proof is quite straightforward. However, if we have to apply many theorems to justify the derived descriptors, then analogy may become the only way to find the correct generalization.

4. CONCLUSION

In this chapter, we have shown the importance of dissimilarities in the process of analogy and shown its interest for incremental learning.

We have developed a system that learns a recognition function of a concept from a set of its examples. This system is called OGUST, from the French: un Outil de Généralisation Utilisant Systématiquement les Théorèmes (Vrain 1987) and it is based on the principle of structural matching (Kodratoff and Ganascia, 1983). This system is not incremental: if we learn a new example after we have obtained a generalization, we are not able to improve our generalization to take into account the new example and we have to start again a generalization of the whole set of examples including the new one. Moreover, if we have a great number of examples, the combinatorial problems are very important, and incremental learning may be a solution to these problems.

The representation of the examples and of the knowledge is based on a subset of first-order logic, containing only predicates of any arity and constants. All the properties of the domain are used in order to learn a generalization of a given set of examples. The justification that an example is really an instance of the obtained generalization may be very complicated and may use a number of theorems.

The system described is currently undergoing two improvements:

— Given a new example, find those it must be compared with in order to draw the most useful analogies.
— The use of the proof that E_1 satisfies a derived descriptor $[A_d = val_d^G]$. For this, a notion of 'similarity between theorems' must be introduced; this similarity takes into account the type of the predicates.

REFERENCES

Carbonell, J. G. (1982) Experimental learning in analogical problem solving. *Proc. of the Second Meeting of the American Association for AI, Pittsburgh, PA*, 1982.

Chouraqui, E. (1985) Construction of a model for reasoning by analogy. In L. Steels and J. A. Campbell (eds.), *Progress in Artificial Intelligence*, Ellis Horwood Ltd., pp. 169–183.

DeJong, G. and Mooney, R. (1986) Explanation based learning: an alternative view. *Machine Learning Journal*, **1** (2), 145–176.

Kodratoff, Y. and Ganascia, J. G. (1986) Improving the generalization step in learning. In R. S. Michalski, J. G. Carbonell and T. M. Mitchell,

Machine Learning, an Artificial Intelligence Approach, vol. II, (eds.), Morgan Kaufmann Publishers, pp. 215–244.

Michalski, R. S. (1983) A theory and methodology of inductive learning. In R. S. Michalski and J. G. Carbonell and T. M. Mitchell (eds.), *Machine Learning, an Artificial Intelligence Approach*, Tioga Publishers Company, pp. 83–129.

Mitchell, T. M., Keller, R., and Kedar-Cabelli, S. (1986) Explanation based generalisation: a unifying view. *Machine Learning Journal*, **1** (1) 47–80.

Vrain, C. (1987) Un outil de généralisation utilisant systématiquement les théorèmes: le système OGUST. *Thèse de troisième cycle soutenue le 25 Février* 1987, Université Paris Sud, Orsay.

4

Architectures for artificial intelligence

J. A. Campbell
Department of Computer Science, University College London,
Gower Street, London WC1E 6BT, UK

SUMMARY

The chapter contains a survey of trends in the design of computer architectures that are suitable for applications in artificial intelligence (AI). In particular, designs for processing LISP, logic programs and rule-based software are considered. Other designs are also examined, where their features are likely to contain general lessons for advances in effectiveness of handling computations that rely on methods of AI.

1. COMPUTING NEEDS OF ARTIFICIAL INTELLIGENCE

There are many competing definitions of artificial intelligence (AI), most of which make some direct or implied reference to 'knowledge' rather than mere 'data'. This reference is a good starting-point for any discussion of what makes the demands of AI on computer architectures different from the demands of conventional computing, because the basic distinctions between knowledge and data are reflected in quite a low-level distinction between typical AI and non-AI computations.

The essence of knowledge is the rich variety of relations or connections established between different data-like pieces of information. During manipulation of knowledge, both the extent of the variety and the number of the relations are either unpredictable or not worth trying to predict. (This is not a fair picture of what may happen *after* the manipulation, e.g. when one is trying to draw lessons or to identify regularities, but that point is not important for the present chapter.) Hence the typical AI data structure is not an array or a similar collection of 'atomic' data where the atoms are stored in a fixed pattern with respect to each other. Instead, the typical structure is looser, allowing the establishment of new connections between atoms and the flexible alteration of existing connections.

This was not the reason why LISP was invented, but it was (and still is) one of the strongest reasons why LISP has always been the most popular programming language for AI. The relevant fact is that LISP is a *pointer-*

based language, allowing easy creation of data structures where the pointers can be used to represent links between facts, concepts, etc. The use of pointers is dynamic, i.e. unlike the situation for conventional languages that permit pointers (e.g. Pascal), the range of possible structures in a computation can be extended at any stage during that computation, and is not limited to what is declared initially by a programmer.

A user refers to pointers directly in LISP whenever there is a call to the function CONS or several standard functions that are almost equally basic. In Prolog, which is the second most popular AI language, the access to pointers is not so direct, but it is implied whenever the infix operator | is used in a clause, and Prolog implementers need pointers to administer basic details of their systems, e.g. in backtracking and structure-sharing.

The same kind of comment as for Prolog can be made in connection with OPS5, a production-rule language which is also popular in some places for AI work such as the development of expert systems. Preconditions and postconditions of rules can refer to pattern-matching on compound data (analogous to the use of | in Prolog) and there are internal features of implementations (e.g. keeping track of the firing of rules) that need to use pointers.

The justification for paying close attention to pointers in hardware design is easiest to see for LISP and least easy for OPS5, among the popular AI languages. There is another consideration, which works the other way round, for AI implementations: *parallelism*. At a given stage of a rule-based computation, in principle the most relevant rule to fire next can be any rule in the set that is accessible to a program. One tries to reduce the size of this problem, in state-of-the-art software systems, by partitioning the rule-base and imposing hierarchies on the knowledge, so that $O(n)$ accesses become $O(\log n)$ accesses, but collection of genuine 'intelligent' knowledge are more messy and do not stay hierarchical for very long. Thus, even if one is focusing on a given rule-set, some inspection of at least the tags or descriptors of other sets is necessary to ensure that the process of chaining over rules is not travelling in an unrewarding or irrelevant direction. Each act of inspection of the preconditions of a rule in a basic production system is independent of all other such acts (even if the consequences are not), so that they can all be carried out in parallel. However, conventional computers require the inspections to occur in sequence, and are thus highly inefficient in this form of computing. An appropriate parallel architecture is needed to make proper use of the form of the computation.

The same comment is true for Prolog, because any mention of a goal in terms of a given functor means that any clause whose head begins with that functor may cause the goal to succeed and therefore deserves to be processed in parallel with all other such clauses. This is described in the Prolog literature as OR-parallelism. AND-parallelism also exists where it is possible to speed up the processing of the body of a clause by examining its components in parallel. The same situation is likely to occur in any other computational logic (e.g. temporal and modal logics) that may be tried out in AI in the future, because logical assertions are essentially declarations about the world that have no procedural or serial meaning unless one is imposed as a secondary property of the system.

LISP is not intrinsically a parallel language, but even at worst it can be subjected to the same kind of treatment that is normal in optimizing conventional numerical programs for vector processors. At best, AI computations that use LISP in the future will increasingly involve distributed or separated actions (e.g. search, cooperative phenomena involving communication through blackboards or message-passing between autonomous objects or actors, and multipurpose computations for speech processing and robotics) which can be handled in parallel with a considerable potential improvement in efficiency. This trend is already occurring, although it is being held back by the fact that the newest LISP hardware designs are quantitative rather than qualitative improvements on earlier designs.

To sum up the foregoing material, the two main ideas distinguishing the needs of AI from non-AI computation are *pointers* and *parallelism*.

If the consequences of this view were simple, we could have designed highly successful AI machines before now by providing large word-lengths and large physical address spaces to service the first idea and multiprocessor configurations to respond to the second. However, life is not so simple.

The 'pointers' mentioned above are conceptual links between pieces of knowledge. Pointers in LISP and other languages to date are bit-patterns specifying addresses in random-access memory (RAM) where information is held. In most cases these patterns *are* the addresses, when they are regarded as integers, i.e. there is no compact encoding, addressing based primarily on the content of what is addressed, etc. However, it is certainly not compulsory for conceptual links to be represented in this very literal and non-AI-like way, which is also a way that is heavily dependent on the traditional von Neumann architecture. One of the limitations of present attempts to fit serious AI computations onto present computers, even computers with non-standard architectures, is that very few of the possibilities inherent in the 'conceptual link' idea (including possibilities for encryptions or encodings which can reduce their size or number) can be exploited in existing hardware designs. A reason for this is that we do not yet have enough systematic experience of it to be able to exploit it very well.

The same is true of parallelism. Unlike the situation for successful routine uses of parallel computing operations, e.g. in supercomputers, steps in an AI computation that are started in parallel because they appear to be independent do not often stay independent for long. An AI computation carried out by multiple agents or processes can be viewed as an exploration of a complex environment in which local discoveries about the structure of the environment by any agent are of global interest for the whole computation (as in individuals' discovery of clues in a collective treasure hunt). Therefore an agent which makes such a discovery needs to transmit it to the other agents, whose behaviour, goals, etc., change when this happens. The result is that the assumption of independence which underlies the use of parellelism is untrue at most stages of the computation, and that the exchanging and interpretation of messages between the supposedly parallel processes slows the computation down to little better than serial speed.

Future large-scale computations in AI will require architectures that can maintain the parallelism that the computations contain while not losing efficiency through being swamped with message-passing activities. In addition, the conceptual links that they manipulate should not be allowed (or forced, in the case of any highly unsuitable architecture) to take a dominant share of the capacity of the architectures.

These two considerations do not cover the whole story when AI architectures are being evaluated, but they provide a strong focus for the evaluation — a necessary service at present, because most surveys of advanced architectures so far have not been *critical* surveys, where the special hardware needs of AI are concerned.

The sections that follow will consider architectures that have properties which improve the efficiency of processing of the popular AI programming languages. They will be followed in turn by more general remarks on AI architectures. This chapter is not intended as a general survey; the instances mentioned are chosen because they illustrate aspects of the views expressed above. Details of other architectures can be found, for example, in material by Treleaven *et al.* (1987), Uhr (1987) and Veen (1986).

2.   LISP-ORIENTED ARCHITECTURES

When contrasted with conventional (numerical, database, etc.) computing, effective processing of LISP programs demands rapid random access to large physical address spaces, minimization of the fraction of storage occupied by pointers, hardware support for simple data-typing, and similar support for stacks (to take account of recursion and of the typical structure of LISP programs, in which relatively large numbers of relatively small functions call each other freely, with the sequence of calls extending to considerable depth).

Special-purpose LISP machines have existed since Greenblatt's original experiments at MIT in 1974. These experiments led to the commercial production of the so-called CADR machine (in 1979) and later LAMBDA by LISP Machines Inc. The best-known of LISP machines is produced by Symbolics Inc., which has its origins in the same MIT LISP milieu. The current commercial product is the Symbolics 3600 series.

The relative successes of these companies and the expansion of public interest in LISP which has followed the popularisation of AI through expert-systems technology have encouraged other companies to enter the market for LISP-oriented machines. The most visible products are the Texas Instruments Explorer and the Xerox 1100 series of computers (lately 1186). In Europe, LISP machine projects with a commercial flavour exist, almost entirely in France. The most distinctive architecture, the MAIA design, has had contributions from the University of Toulouse (Sansonnet, 1984), the Compagnie Générale d'Electricité (CGE-Marcoussis) and the Centre

National d'Etudes des Télécommunications, and is available through the company AMAIA-Bayonne.

The discussion below will consider mainly the Symbolics 3600 and MAIA designs, and will touch on others (including non-commercial machines) where these can illustrate desirable features of LISP hardware.

As a language, LISP offers little general scope for parallel processing. Of course, it is possible to find computations specified within non-trivial AI programs that can be performed in parallel, but exploiting these aspects is not (in our present state of understanding) a hardware exercise. Therefore it is not surprising that a standard feature of a LISP architecture is a single central processor, i.e. a conventional solution. There are some departures from this choice in work on devices or software suitable for multiprocessing in LISP, e.g. in the Scheme-81 chip project (Batali et al., 1982) the latest (LAMBDA) design from LISP Machines Inc., the EVLIS experimental hardware at the University of Osaka and the development of Multilisp (Halstead, 1985), but the question of how to write LISP programs to make good use of the resulting freeedom is still open.

Where multiple processors exist in LISP machines whose designs are now stable, the common tendency is to have two units, one to handle execution of the user's program and one for memory management. The second processor is an answer to the problem of pointer-intensive demands on storage which has been mentioned above. An essential feature of memory management is garbage collection, or freeing of storage for further use when the information that it contains is no longer referenced or referenceable by a computation. Cohen (1981) has surveyed the issues and the alternative general techniques for garbage collection. In traditional computers, any time and resources that a central processor devotes to garbage collection are taken away from the servicing of a user's program. The moving of responsibility for memory management to a second processor is therefore an obvious and highly desirable way of increasing the efficiency of a LISP machine.

The MAIA workstation architecture is probably the simplest conceivable example of a machine adapted to practical computing with LISP, lists (any data structures whose parts are linked together by pointers) and pointers. It is shown in Fig. 1.

The arrows leading from the bus indicate possible connections to special-purpose interfaces, e.g. for networking. The graphic processor is not a requirement of efficient computing in LISP, but it is a reasonable concession to the modern fashion for bit-mapped graphical displays. At the level of effective presentation of information for users, these displays have expanded the scope of what can be done through computations in AI. However, because the flexibility of their manipulations typically requires operations on list structures, they also make heavy demands on RAM. (For example, for a long time it was a piece of folklore among intensive LISP users that a workstation would need 2 megabytes (MB) of RAM to support serious LISP applications in AI, symbolic mathematical computing, etc. The folklore has now adapted to the fact that 8 MB is common, and needed, on

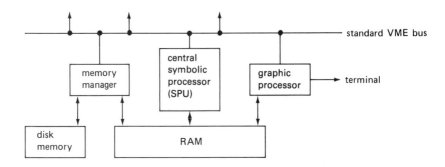

Fig. 1 — MAIA architecture.

such machines, whether LISP machines or the more conventional designs represented by Sun and DEC products. The change can be explained completely by the transition from character- and line-oriented displays to bit-mapped graphics.) It is therefore appropriate to hand over the specialized book-keeping of graphics to a separate processor, so that the kind of computing that is central to the 'AI' of a problem can be performed, without distractions, by at least one special-purpose device.

There are many varieties of architectures with the same general features as Fig. 1, but with differences in detail. The most common differences are in the means of communication of the central processor with RAM (e.g. connection via a bus rather than directly) and in the nature of additional processing devices attached to the main bus.

An example of bus connection between memory and a central processor is the Symbolics 3600 architecture shown in Fig. 2. The IFU and IC sections

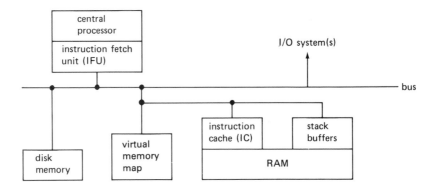

Fig. 2 — Symbolics 3600 architecture.

play the same part here as in conventional architectures with pipelining, caching and look-ahead features to speed up serial processing. The virtual memory map and the stack buffers are discussed later.

Designs such as Fig. 1 and Fig. 2 are hidden inside more complicated structures in many other computers, e.g. the Xenologic X-1 (Ribler, 1987). However, the extra complication is typically due to the provision for add-on units to expand the RAM capacity or to integrate the machine into the configuration of a host machine which acts as a front end (good examples that are new in 1987 are the Xenologic X-1, which can be attached to Sun workstations in this way, and the Integrated Inference Machines S45000), or both.

If all of a large RAM space is to be equally usable, then a pointer must be equally capable of pointing to any place (i.e. representing the address of any word) in the memory. Hence, if the memory contains 2^n words, an individual word which may hold a pointer should be at least n bits long. The actual length should allow for representation of pointers, plus bits for error-checking and marker bits to help in the administration of garbage collection and the indication of types of data. Therefore the length of a word is an important issue in the design in LISP-oriented machines, and it is common to find that these lengths are greater than for conventional computers. For example, the Symbolics 3600 uses a 44-bit word, with 6 bits being available for (type) tagging of data, 28 bits for pointers, and 2 bits for CDR coding (see below). The MAIA machine has a 40-bit word.

The traditional way of storing LISP information in a word (McCarthy *et al.*, 1962) is to regard the word as being divided into two equal-sized parts (plus additional bits for the administrative functions mentioned above), with each part being capable of holding one pointer. This approach is now out of fashion in LISP machine designs because of the extremely long words that it needs. The newer fashion is to provide the same space by calling on two-word blocks. Moreover, it is not necessary to represent each pointer in full, because studies of the running of LISP programs have shown that most pointers are of two rather trivial kinds: NIL (indicating the end of a list) and a pointer from the current word W in storage to the next word W+1. Therefore the meaning of a word whose pointer field contains information x depends on the meaning of the CDR-coding entry in that word. If the coding indicates NIL, then x is the last item in a list. If the coding indicates 'next', then x is an element in the list, and the next element of the list is found in word W+1. Otherwise, x is to be read as a pointer to the word in storage where the next element can be found. This simple idea greatly improves the handling of the scarce resource of RAM in computations (in Prolog and OPS5 as well as LISP) that rely heavily on lists, but it is not yet universal in LISP machine designs.

This is an example of a property of list processing which may be obvious in retrospect but which needed non-trivial experimental observations of LISP programs in order to be confirmed. Although we have now accumulated much experience in LISP, it is possible to believe that further insights into LISP behaviour, with implications for improvements in the design of

LISP hardware, are still possible. As an indication of this view, the most extensive tabulation of performance figures for different machines on a set of LISP benchmark tests (Gabriel, 1985) contains unexpected features (e.g. for superficially similar tests A and B, machine X performs noticeably better than machine Y on A, but Y outperforms X on B) that are still not understood.

Administration of virtual memory, as in the 'memory map' function in Fig. 2, is a common need in overall memory management for LISP-oriented machines. As for conventional computers, virtual memory is a means of making the user believe that the RAM space in a computer is larger than it is. This is achieved by paging or segmentation methods for automatic exchange of material between RAM and disk storage. Virtual memory is not a concept with some deep foundation in computer science; it is a technological fix for an economic problem. The problem is that RAM has been very expensive and disk storage has been relatively cheap, while many computations' demands for RAM (not just in AI) have exceeded the supply. However, the argument of cost is becoming less serious with time. Use of virtual memory in conventional computations, where pointers are not the central feature of data structures, is a painless way of living with past technology. Where pointers are crucial, it is grossly inefficient. Heavy use of virtual memory in large-scale AI is a disaster. In future AI hardware designs, it should be avoided at all costs. One possible way forward, architecturally, is the outline of Garcia Molina et al. (1984) for a machine with a RAM of up to 10^{10} bytes of storage.

The 'stack buffer' feature that is shown in Fig. 2 is present in some form in most LISP machine designs, although the choice of its location is not fixed. The basic reason for having a hardware mechanism to deal with stacks is that the LISP evaluation model makes heavy use of these structures, e.g. for keeping track of control flow in an executing program and for administering bindings of values to variables. Moreover, the issues that are raised in LISP persist even for other AI languages: in AI, non-trivial problem-solving is always likely to require the creation of contexts in which complex information about bindings and the state of incomplete computation directed towards achieving goals in the problem-solving process can be held. Rapid switching between contexts is also necessary. Hence it will always be desirable to support this activity, which is essentially stack-based, in hardware.

Although it belongs in the same general family that is described by Fig. 1, the Scheme-81 chip design (Batali et al., 1982) has three additional features that are significant for LISP and for AI computation in general. The first is that the monolithic 'central processor' facility is broken down into frequently-used primitives related to common basic list-processing operations, e.g. the LISP functions EVAL, MEMQ, CAR, CDR, RPLACA and RPLACD. These functions are implemented either (in the case of EVAL and MEMQ) in the purpose-built hardware units attached to a special bus or (e.g. for the other four functions) through protocols implemented in the bus itself and acting on list data read from memory in situations where the data are pieces of programs to be executed. The second novel development is that hardware stacks are associated with individual hardware units that need them; for example, each register R available to EVAL has an associated stack, onto which information in R is pushed when it is about to be overwritten. The third novelty is that the RAM is partitioned into separate memory units attached to a common memory bus, with the idea that separate Scheme chips linked together may call on each other's local memory on occasions to solve large problems by collective and probably parallel computing on subproblems. To assist in this process, some of the bits available in any Scheme pointer can be used to refer to non-local memory units. This architecture should at least encourage experiments in non-local and collective LISP computing, although it is not a cure for the problems of parallelism mentioned in the previous section, which are likely to show up as bottlenecks caused by excessive traffic on the memory bus.

3. ARCHITECTURES FOR PROGRAMMING IN LOGIC

The adoption of Prolog as the key language for the Japanese 'Fifth Generation' computing project has caused considerable activity in the design and construction of Prolog machines. At the same time, some of the activity has the broader target of designing machines that are efficient for logics more general than the restricted form of first-order predicate calculus used in Prolog.

The Japanese interest in logic-programming hardware has been responsible for the idea of rating hardware performance in logical inferences per second (LIPS) rather than arithmetical operations per second. The first target of the Fifth Generation project was the building of a personal sequential inference (PSI) machine, essentially a Prolog workstation, with a performance of about 30K LIPS. This target has been reached, and the production of the PSI machine is now the responsibility of the Mitsubishi company. According to Japanese reports, more than 100 have been built so far. The next target is a parallel inference machine (PIM) module, with a performance of 3M LIPS, which can be linked together in groups of at least 10 for parallel processing. The PIM work is apparently on schedule at present. A subsequent target is a cooperative high-speed inference (CHI) machine with a performance in the 100M–1000M LIPS range, using a PSI2 architecture (PSI design, speeded up by about a factor of 5) as the front-end seen by a user.

The Japanese architectures in this set are organized around hardware implementation of the presumed basic operation of logic programming, which is unification (Robinson, 1977). This involves finding consistent substitutions for variables, where such substitutions are possible, between two logical assertions. The process of resolution uses this information to obtain the most general logical consequence of the two assertions, i.e. to make one logical inference. Because of the structure of Prolog programs, inferences on different parts of the programs can proceed naturally in parallel. The Japanese (and other) logic programming architectures therefore contain unification processors or more general (but still single) processing elements (PEs) which receive inference tasks from a pool or a controller. In all but PSI, there are explicit multiple PEs. If there is no central pool, it is common for each PE to keep a copy of the entire program and to act on only a small part of it following a command from the controller. Unification is a simple algorithmic pattern-matching exercise which needs no extended or contextual data.

The PSI architecture is shown in Fig. 3 (Yokota *et al.*, 1983). If the part A is regarded as RAM and B as a central processor, Fig. 3 shows that the

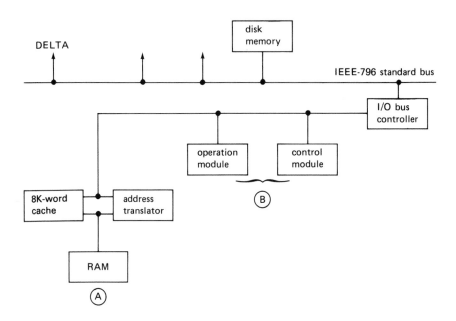

Fig. 3 — PSI architecture.

functional architecture is quite conventional. The unconventional features are contained in the Prolog-oriented details of the microprogramming of B, which is organized around support for unification and for the backtracking that takes place when it is found to be impossible to satisfy a given Prolog clause. For example, B has large register-like internal storage to hold frequently-accessed control information, multiple stack facilities, and the ability to administer up to 63 concurrently-executing processes.

The RAM can contain up to 16M 40-bit words, of which 32 bits are available for data pointers, 6 bits for indicating types, and 2 bits for garbage-collector administration. At this low level of detail, the information being processed by a typical Prolog machine has the same 'list' character as LISP information. The choice of the wordlength and the meanings for groupings of bits is therefore governed by the same general considerations as for LISP architectures.

The arrows on the IEEE-796 bus indicate connections to typical I/O devices. In addition, the label DELTA indicates the possibility of attachment of PSI to a relational database machine of that name which is being developed in another part of the Fifth Generation project. (AI assistance for more effective use of conventional databases is an important target of the overall project).

The PIM architecture consists of multiple (e.g. ten) modules of the simple form shown in Fig. 4, each connected directly to a network con-

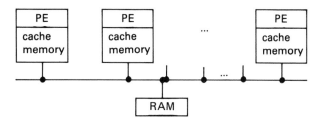

Fig. 4 — PIM architecture.

troller. A module contains eight PE+cache elements. Its 3M LIPS performance, which is a speed-up of 100 over PSI performance, is obtained essentially by providing in parallel hardware what PSI provides in serial handling of concurrency.

The raw speed of architectures in this family scales up with size, but this effect also suggests that raw speed is a misleading indicator of power in solving AI problems. For example, many things can be inferred in a large logical system, but only a small number of them will be relevant for a particular problem. Moreover, the more interesting the problem, the less it will be possible to write the criteria for 'interest' into static or unchanging parts of a program before that program runs. In practice, negotiation or intercommunication between parts of a program will be needed, and the most effective way of linking PEs to minimize traffic bottlenecks is then not clear. At the least, this question requires extensive simulation or testing, and is a good open topic for research.

There are many examples of alternative Prolog machine designs, particularly in Japan: most of these are no more than feasibility studies. An exception, which illustrates the 'pool' idea mentioned at the beginning of this section and which is still being developed, is the Fujitsu KABU-WAKE architecture (Sohma et al., 1985), which is shown in Fig. 5. The 'CONT' and data networks are circular, the two points A are the same point, and this is also true for B. The network contains 15 PEs plus one element reserved for I/O.

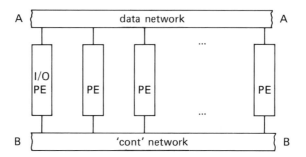

Fig. 5 — KABU-WAKE architecture.

Each PE holds a copy of the entire Prolog program, and starts by processing a part of the program by depth-first search, i.e. if the part contains the clauses a(...):- b(...), c(...). and a(...):- d(...), e(...)., then its PE will concentrate on a depth-first search to try to satisfy b(...). When such a search succeeds, the PE is idle, and sends notification of that fact to other PEs within the CONT ring. A busy PE receiving this notification splits its longest-lived current job in half and sends the relevant half to the idle PE via the data network. For example, a PE which is processing b(...) above would answer the request by giving the idle PE the job of trying to satisfy a(...) by examining the clause containing d and e. The right overall result of a run can be recovered from the partial results through use of tagging to indicate where and when each partial task has originated.

A considerable advantage of this architecture, on paper, is that the parallel capability of the system can be used automatically to the best extent: idle-processor time is kept to a minimum, and the method of transferring new tasks to PEs ensures that the system never overloads itself. Designs with this type of property are therefore likely to be useful in general AI applications, not merely in processing of Prolog problems.

The special characteristics of Prolog machines are based on hardware support for unification, which is the primitive operation that makes rapid Prolog inferences possible. Other logical schemes use other formal properties as a basis for their inference procedures. If any such property has a chance of being efficient for large-scale computation, it can be used as the foundation of a computer architecture. A good example is the connection method (Bibel and Buchberger, 1985), which works for the full first-order predicate calculus, and which relies on the property that any formula written in an appropriate form is true if and only if every 'path' through the formula contains a literal (essentially a Boolean variable) and its negation (a path is a set of literals, containing just one from each clause in the formula): a machine based on this method would be capable of setting up and checking all paths, and should use a high degree of parallelism. A prototype machine has been built, using repeated copies of a small number of functional elements which can act as reconfigurable switches with small amounts of local memory and computing power.

4.   ARCHITECTURES FOR PROCESSING RULE-BASED INFORMATION

The most relevant property of rule bases in AI, for computation, is not that suitably chosen subsets of rules should be searched in parallel at each step (although this is clearly part of the story). It is that, because only one rule is chosen for firing in a typical step, the overall state of the rule base, RAM, etc., does not change very much from step to step. This insight, obtained from extensive experiments with the OPS5 production-rule language, has led to the development of the so-called RETE algorithm (Forgy, 1982) for pattern matching and computations on rule bases. Versions of this algorithm are used not only on special architectures but in some expert system implementations on conventional machines.

Appropriate architectures for processing rule bases should be capable of using the RETE algorithm effectively, and should also contain both parallel-processing facilities, e.g. in order to search rule sets in parallel for interesting properties), and some form of hierarchical structuring (to assist in the representation of rules in partitioned sets). The three architectures considered below do not seem to have been designed with all of these considerations in mind at the same time, but they are better adapted to the processing of rules than any of the architectures considered in the previous sections.

Conceptually the simplest of the three is the ZMOB architecture developed at the University of Maryland. Its basic structure is the same as in Fig. 5, but with one of the two communication rings removed. The earliest version of ZMOB (Rieger *et al.*, 1981) contained 256 PEs and one external-interface processor. Each PE has a Z80 microcomputer with 64K bytes of memory. The local flow of control in ZMOB involves the passing of messages on the ring; the typical message is 48 bits long, of which 16 bits are used for contents and 12 bits for destination information. The total of 28 bits in principle allows a variety of patterns to be sent: the most interesting types of messages are broadcasts of the form 'act if you recognize this pattern' rather than messages to fixed destinations. ZMOB is intended as a general-purpose parallel processor rather than a specialized AI machine, but its model of computation has advantages for AI, and for the processing of rule sets in particular. Its topology is nevertheless likely to be a limiting factor because it does not allow hierarchical representations and the RAM capacity of individual PEs is rather small for anything in AI except rather passive responses to messages or pattern-directed broadcasts.

Hierarchical organization is the main structural property of the DADO machine (Stolfo *et al.*, 1983), which has been built at Columbia University. This contains a network of processors (Intel 8751s, each with 4K bytes of EPROM and 16K of RAM) arranged in a binary tree. Each node of the tree also contains three links with a width of 8 bits. One of the links connects a node to its parent in the tree, and the other two (except in leaf nodes) connect with the node's descendants.

In operation, the tree consists of three conceptual levels. At the lowest level, nodes store information about individual rules. A rule may therefore be represented across a low-level subtree. In the middle or production memory (PM) level, each node 'stores' a single rule, i.e. it is the root node of a subtree that represents this rule. The highest level provides the control and permits broadcasts of requests to the PM level. A cycle consists of three steps. In the first, the top level broadcasts information about a target pattern to be matched, and each PM initiates matching of this pattern to information in its subtree. Each PM computes a rating based on the goodness of the match. In the second step, each node holding a rating sends it in parallel to its parent, which chooses the better of the two ratings that it receives and sends this result one level higher up the tree. When the winning rating reaches the next node, the PM responsible for this rating is instructed to send the postcondition of its rule to the root. The root then determines what general updates to the rule set are needed and broadcasts instructions to all PMs to make the appropriate changes in parallel. The root is now ready to initiate the next cycle.

As an indication of the performance, the DADO group estimates that a ten-level tree consisting of 1023 Motorola 68000 PEs, each with 64K bytes of RAM, should be capable of 13 000 rule-firing cycles per second.

While the DADO machine is obviously specialized to the processing of rules, another Columbia University project is much more flexible. This is NON-VON (Shaw, 1981), which uses 'small processing elements' (SPEs) in the same binary tree structure as DADO, but with additional components which make it into a promising general-purpose design. NON-VON also contains large processing elements (LPEs), which are standard 32-bit commercial microprocessors (e.g. Motorola 68020) and a 'significant amount' (Shaw, 1987) of RAM plus a disk drive. SPE leaf nodes are arranged in a square grid pattern, with each leaf being connected to four nearest-neighbour leaves. Each LPE is connected to one SPE at a high level in the SPE tree, as shown in Fig. 6. Finally, the LPEs themselves are joined together in a 'two-stage' topology in an LPE network. The machine can be linked to a host or front-end computer from a point in this network. Typically, the LPEs broadcast instructions to their SPE subtrees for execution in parallel, using as much of the hierarchical structure of the subtrees as convenient.

Unusually for AI machine projects, the performance of NON-VON has been assessed on a wide range of problems and the assessment is easily available (Shaw, 1987). For example, the performance on processing of production rules suggests that a NON-VON machine with 2048 SPEs (on eight-SPE custom chips) and 33 LPEs, which would have a cost between the prices of a DEC VAX 11/780 and a DEC 2060, would handle rule-firings between 200 and 900 times faster than a VAX 11/780 running a LISP program embodying the RETE algorithm. Shaw's paper also claims super-

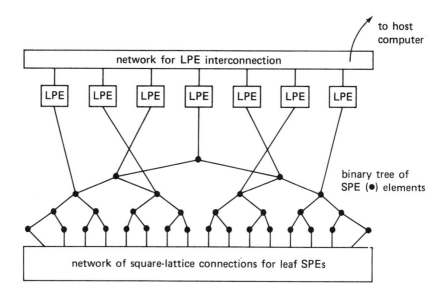

Fig. 6 — NON-VON architecture.

ior performance of NON-VON (at least as good as specialized equipment, e.g. the ICL content-addressable file store) on database computations.

The general lesson of the NON-VON design is that flexible computation in unconventional structures requires combinations of PEs and interconnections which are chosen after careful modelling of the basic computing operations which are to be carried out. In particular, it is unlikely that a simple topology will be both good and flexible.

5. SIGNIFICANT ARCHITECTURES FOR OTHER PURPOSES

The same kinds of lessons that can be learned from the NON-VON system are available from other architectures. The material in this section will be presented in the form of notes (because of the pressure of space) that summarize the particular issues that each architecture illustrates.

5.1 Connection machine (Hillis, 1985)

The basic topology of this machine (built commercially by Thinking Machines Inc.) is a square lattice, with PEs connected to their four nearest neighbours. In addition, there is a general intercommunication network that can connect the PEs in arbitrary patterns; this allows for long-distance connections to be set up. The prototype Connection Machine had 2^{16} PEs; it is possible to order a 2^{20}-PE machine with the help of a large amount of money. A typical PE has 512 bytes of RAM. A front-end or host computer can communicate with the Connection Machine in a conventional way, via a memory bus. In addition, large-scale I/O can be achieved at a high rate (500M bits per second) through a separate channel.

The processing and storage power of a PE are well balanced, although both of these are quite small. Hence typical AI information must be spread over an extended area of PEs, and updating, searches, etc., take place through the passing of simple messages. Even though this design seems to break information down into pieces that are too small to represent items of 'knowledge', Hillis (1985) makes some persuasive qualitative arguments that the design is well adapted to AI.

The primary programming language for the machine is a version of LISP, in which there is an additional data structure called a xector -'roughly a set of PEs with a value stored in each PE'. The language includes two operators, α (which turns an expression into a xector) and β (which applies to two-argument functions, and turns them into functions that can reduce a xector to an ordinary S-expression, or (with two xectors as arguments) sends the values of the first xector to the indexes given by the second). With just these two extensions, LISP can exploit all the routing power and the structuring that is contained in the architecture.

The Connection Machine is applicable to many problems outside AI: in fact, any problems for which LISP or the regular structure of the hardware are specially well adapted. For example, the xector representation allows counting, traversing, merging, etc., operations on compound items of size n to be achieved in O ($\log n$) time, and sorting in time $O(\log^2 n)$.

The original intention behind the design was to provide support for the semantic-net form of knowledge representation in AI. In this respect, it was inspired by the earlier NETL architecture (Fahlman, 1979), which had a superficially similar topology and which relied on the assumption that set intersection would be the basic operation needed in semantic-net processing.

5.2 Cellular automata

The most extreme form (in simplicity) of a design using a square lattice is one in which each PE contains one bit of information, and updates this infor-mation at each cycle of the machine according to rules that take as input the contents of some or all of the neighbouring PEs. This is exactly the model for a cellular automaton, which can be considered (on paper) along with Turing machines, Post production systems, etc., as a simple scheme for determining properties of computation in general. Recently, at least one architecture has been built to behave as a cellular automaton (Toffoli and Margolus, 1987). This so-called CAM machine is already in use for experiments in modelling of physical processes (e.g. Navier–Stokes equation) and the mathematics of dynamical systems. However, it seems to be also a useful tool for modelling low-level details of possible AI architectures. The CAM-6 'machine' is a plug-in board that can be attached to an IBM PC or compatible computer, having at least 256K bytes of RAM, and is available for about $1500 from Systems Concepts Inc. of San Francisco. This may be the most cost-effective way of entering the field of simulation of AI architectures!

5.3   BBN Butterfly

This machine is of interest because it is in regular use and is commercially available. Its basic PEs each contain a Motorola 68000 processor plus local RAM with a capacity that can be as low as 256K and as high as 4M bytes. Each PE has a 'co-processor' that is responsible for communication between it and a switch. Groups of four PEs are connected to each switch, and switches are conceptually arranged on two parallel lines. Each switch on a line has connections to four other switches: the one directly opposite it and three adjacent switches, all in the opposite line.

The earliest applications of the Butterfly system have been in parallel numerical processing. However, as a possible AI system it resembles several of the architectures mentioned above. It should therefore help in the evaluation of alternative topologies, e.g. if systematic measurements are made of its performance on tests or benchmarks that are also run on rival architectures such as NON-VON and the Connection Machine.

5.4   ALICE (Darlington and Reeve, 1981)

ALICE is an Imperial College project, originally intended as a design for efficient functional programming by graph-reduction methods. It is of interest here mainly because its conceptual structure fits some obvious ideas on the structure of general AI computations, e.g. the division of problems into subproblems that can be handed out non-hierarchically to a pool of PEs. Structurally the design looks like an extension of the KABU-WAKE architecture (Fig. 5), but where there is an additional type of element, A 'packet-pool segment' (PPS) attached to the DATA network. An idle PE looks for a PPS that needs updating, decides whether it can perform this operation, and places an updated PPS back into the pool if the operation is performed. A PE can access the DATA network either by calling a specific PPS or by inspecting the circulation of PPSs around the communication rings that are a part of that network.

The ALICE machine is now working. Assessment of its performance on AI-like tasks should be valuable in allowing the appropriateness of a 'processor pool and task pool' architectural model to be determined. In theory it is highly appropriate but in practice it may suffer from the same kinds of communication bottlenecks that have been mentioned earlier in this chapter.

6.   CONCLUDING REMARKS

The subject of architectures for AI needs a much longer chapter to do justice to all the designs that exist. This is possibly a tribute to the health and vigour of the subject, although it is possibly also a consequence of the absence of any generally-agreed methodology for comparing or even classifying alternative designs. This is the biggest gap in the subject: only a few publications (e.g. Uhr (1987), Deering (1984), Hillis (1985), Shaw (1987)) make any moves towards filling it. Therefore there are plenty of opportunities for future research. The study of architectures is a good topic for any ambitious graduate student in AI.

Architectures and architectural trends that are not covered above but which would deserve detailed attention in a longer chapter include:

— *'Connectionist'* and *neural-net designs*, which derive their inspiration from speculations about the way in which a brain functions or 'ought' to function. (The manifesto of this school of thought is the book by Rumelhart and McClelland (1986), and a net-like architecture on a board that can be attached to an IBM PC AT is 'AI-NET 101', available for $4500 (with software) from AI Ware Inc. of Cleveland, Ohio).

— The *MIDAS* architecture (Maples and Logan, 1986), which is interesting because it combines a pyramidal interconnection scheme for processors with a shared RAM and the possibility of reconfiguration.

— The *IX* architecture (Higuchi *et al.*, 1985), a Japanese design planned around effective implementations of semantic-net storage and operations, which is also pyramidal in its organization of PEs. IX is apparently not just a small-scale experiment and is being expanded from its original configuration of 16 PEs.

— Design of *hybrid machines* in which parts are optimized for one particular form of processing that is relevant for AI (e.g. logic programming, object-oriented computing, pattern matching). The Japanese NTT *ELIS* architecture (Takeuchi *et al.*, 1983) is one example of the trend; the newest example is the large *SPAN* project in the EEC ESPRIT programme, which started in 1987 and in which University College London is strongly involved.

— The possibility of using the *Transputer*, produced by Inmos Ltd in the UK, as a basic and not very expensive component for building almost arbitrary AI architectures.

— The advisability of considering the use of *graph theory* as an essential tool for analysis and design of connections in any AI architecture.

REFERENCES

Batali, J. *et al.* (1982) The Scheme-81 architecture-system and chip. *Proc. 1982 Conf. on Adv. Res. in VLSI, Massachusetts Institute of Technology*, pp. 69–77.

Bibel, W. and Buchberger, B. (1985) *Future Generation Comp. Sys.* **1**, 177.

Cohen, J. (1981) *ACM Computing Surveys* **13**, 341.

Darlington, J. and Reeve, M. (1981) *Proc. Int. Symp. on Functional Prog. Languages and Comput. Arch.*, pp. 32–62.

Deering, M. F,. (1984) *Proc. AAAI-84, Austin, Texas*, pp. 73–78.

Fahlman, S. E. (1979) *NETL: a System for Representing and Using Real-World Knowledge*, MIT Press, Cambridge, MA.

Forgy, C. L. (1982) *Artificial Intelligence* **19** 17.

Gabriel, R. P. (1985) *Performance and Evaluation of LISP Systems*, MIT Press, Cambridge, MA.

Garcia Molina, H., Lipton, R. J. and Valdes, J. (1984) *IEEE Trans. Comput.* **33**, 391.

Halstead, R. H. (1985) *ACM Trans. on Prog. Lang. and Syst.* **7**, 501.

Higuchi, T. *et al.* (1985) *Proc. 1985 EUROMICRO Symp.*, North-Holland, Amsterdam, pp. 95–104.

Hillis, W. D. (1985) *The Connection Machine*, MIT Press, Cambridge, MA.

Maples, C. and Logan, D. (1986) In: A. Wouk (ed.) *New Computing Environments: Parallel, Vector, Systolic,* Society for Industrial and Applied Mathematics, Philadelphia, pp. 154–178.

McCarthy, J. *et al.* (1962) *LISP 1.5 Programmer's Manual,* MIT Press, Cambridge, MA.

Rieger, C. *et al.* (1981) *Proc. 7th Int. Joint Conf. on AI, Vancouver,* pp. 955–960.

Robinson, J. A. (1977) *Logic — Form and Function,* Edinburgh University Press, Edinburgh.

Rumelhart, D. E. and McClelland, J. L. (1986) *Parallel Distributed Processing: Explorations in the Microstructure of Cognition,* Vol. 1, *Foundations,* MIT Press, Cambridge, MA.

Sansonnet, J. P. (1984) *Technique et Science Informatiques* **3**, 397.

Shaw, D. E. (1981) *Proc. 7th Int. Joint Conf. on AI, Vancouver,* pp. 961–963.

Shaw, D. E. (1987) *Artificial Intelligence* **32**, 151.

Sohma, Y. *et al.* (1985) *Proc. IFIP TC-10 Working Conf. on Fifth Generation Comput. Arch., UMIST, Manchester.*

Stolfo, S. J. *et al.* (1983) *Proc. 8th Int. Joint Conf. on AI, Karlsruhe,* pp. 850–854.

Takeuchi, I. *et al.* (1983) *ACM SIGPLAN Notices* **18** (7).

Toffoli, T. and Margolus, N. (1987) *Cellular Automata Machines: a New Environment for Modelling,* MIT Press, Cambridge, MA.

Treleaven, P. C., Refenes, A. N., Lees, K. J., and McCabe, S. C. (1987) *Computer Architectures for Artificial Intelligence.* In: P. C. Treleaven and M. Vaneschi (eds.) *Future Parallel Computers,* Springer-Verlag, Berlin, pp. 416–492.

Uhr, L. (1987) *Multi-Computer Architectures for Artificial Intelligence,* John Wiley & Sons Inc., New York.

Veen, A. H. (1986) *ACM Computing Surveys* **18**, 365.

Yokota, M. *et al.* (1983) New Generation Computing **1** (2).

Part II
AI methods in decision support

5

Knowledge-based systems for aid in decision-making: methodology and examples

José Cuena
Facultad de Informática, Universidad Politécnica, Km 7,
Carretera de Valencia, 28031 Madrid, Spain

1. INTRODUCTION

The expert system concept meant, apart from the possibility of transferring the knowledge of expert persons to a computer, the introduction of a new architecture of computer applications in which appear separately the knowledge and the process for interpreting it.

With this architecture not only can systems be designed that model the knowledge of expert persons, but also all those for whom it may be possible to define a construction methodology of their knowledge base as well as an interpretation procedure. This idea widens the field of possibilities of this concept, allowing its application in areas in which formulable knowledge is available, proceeding from mathematical theories or mathematical models of a classical type.

An important field of application is that of decision making, traditionally supported by operations-research techniques in which an important stock of techniques exist that would allow their use in knowledge-based systems.

The purpose of the present chapter is to propose a general structure of this type of system, as well as a possible methodology for building its knowledge base. It is important to point out at the same time that the use of this knowledge-based system concept will give rise to wide range of specific architectures adapted to the class of problems to be solved and so to the classification of the knowledge to be modelled, in which it will be possible to handle varied pieces of knowledge, of both a procedural and a declarative kind. Therefore it can be predicted that, in the near future, knowledge-based systems will not be treated in general terms but by classes, according to their objectives and formal aspects of their knowledge.

Two case studies are also presented, in outline: traffic control and flood prediction.

2. THE DECISION-MAKING PROBLEM

The knowledge to support a decision based on real-time data must be able to provide answers to the following questions:

(a) 'What happens?': that is, it must be capable of analysing a situation, identifying advantageous and problematic aspects.
(b) 'What can happen?': ability to reason on the evolution of the system, with the control decisions remaining constant, in the problematic aspects or in the advantageous ones in such a way that it might be possible to identify the possible descriptive patterns of the situation in future moments.
(c) 'What should be done?': ability to reason on the control actions most convenient for improving the results of the system's operation. This aspect is, therefore, the support of the decisions, but it requires the two previous ones for its adequate grounding.

Given the characteristics of the knowledge to be modelled, in general, not all of it can be obtained from expert judgement. It is, in effect, possible to identify knowledge of type (a) from expert persons, since it is made up of assessment judgements; however, in type (b) knowledge, when the systems for which a forecast is being made have a significant degree of complexity, it is difficult (based on personal conjectures) to be able to build up directly a reasoning process on the final aspects of the system evolution. In this case, the expert's knowledge can provide theories to explain the evolution, judgements to estimate the parameters and valuations on the reliability of the results when they are applied, even estimates for distinguishing among several applicable theories according to the type of problem to be analysed. Therefore, for type (b) knowledge, two levels are identified, a basic one of instrumentation of the behaviour theories of a system and another one for system evaluation and control. Something similar can be said of type (c) knowledge. Although an expert can have ideas on the type of actions to be applied in order to solve or alleviate certain types of problem, it is not easy to identify directly groups of detailed actions for each problem which, at the same time, are consistent among themselves; it is therefore admissible to establish a knowledge representation based on a simplified inference version of the simulation model integrated into a general frame of reasoning contributed by human experts.

These considerations can be summarized in the idea of integration of the technical knowledge included in the simulation model of the system together with the judgements and handling knowledge of this model by expert persons.

This has, in effect, been the scheme which has been used in classic modelling applications:

— A set of simulation models of the different aspects of behaviour integrated from a data viewpoint so that its application in sequence is possible.
— One or several expert persons who try out different scenarios and

decision options with the models and identify the more convenient ones and even carry out sensitivity analyses by studying modelling parameters and judgements.

The proposed system attempts the integration into a single computable structure not only of the model's knowledge but also that of the person using it. The advantage of this type of application is its possibility for use in real time for the management of complex systems, since while the scheme based on separated models and human experts can contribute to greater quality levels, it cannot be operative in daily decision making, which limits the interest of this type of application.

In order to arrive at this type of system based on a mixed mathematical model and human expert knowledge, it is necessary to accept restrictions in the quality of representation of both sources of knowledge. In order to reduce simulation-model knowledge to inferential schemes, a line of abstraction of the classic numerical techniques in qualitative terms has been created, initially launched by Hayes and later followed by de Kleer, Brown and Forbus, among others.

3. AN ARCHITECTURE OF KNOWLEDGE-BASED SYSTEMS FOR AID IN DECISION MAKING

The structuring principles of a knowledge base must be the reasoning patterns that are going to be used in solving the goal problems of the base. The problems to be solved for decision making are related to the abstract concept of systems management. For this purpose a system can be defined as a set of interrelated components that together produce a final behaviour. In an abstract system of this type the following can be distinguished:

— The external actions provoked by:
  • The environment in which the system operates.
  • The decisions of those responsible for the system's management.
— The operation of the system produced by the incidence of some components on others in such a way that the change of state of one of them has an effect on the others.
— The valuation for decision purposes of the system operation, that is, the assessment of the measures of adjustment to possible management goals.

The management of the system is established by reasoning about:

— Evolution of external actions (scenario definition).
— Behaviour of the system faced with the different forseeable scenarios in different decision patterns.
— Identification of actual and forseeable problems.

As has already been indicated, there exists a set of techniques for treating these problems, from the operations research field:

— Black-box-type models for representing the development of the external actions (time series, regression analysis, for example).
— Simulation models to represent the system's behaviour. In this field, according to the types, there are several different approaches: discrete models of state change for the management processes, that can also be dealt with by queueing theory, models of finite-difference type obtained from the partial derivatives of the physical laws of the phenomenon to be dealt with and, finally, models of finite elements formulated directly in order to discretize the physical behaviour of continuous media.
— Mathematical programming models in order to obtain directly the best decisions with respect to objective functions, imposed by the absence of problems and the presence of all advantages.

With these tools, the management expert tries out different modelling options and even objective functions and as a consequence obtains criteria for decision-making. This reasoning concept can be represented as knowledge base with the following components:

— A forecasting base that incorporates the knowledge elements for estimating the possible forms of future evolution of the external actions to the system. This base could also embody procedural elements in the different representation options.
— A qualitative simulation base that deduces the system's behaviour patterns caused by the possible environmental actions.
— A problem identification base which, from the registered and forecast behaviours, deduces the likelihood of the problematic aspects.
— A decision planning base that first identifies the individualized decisions in order to alleviate or solve every problem and, secondly, uses other knowledge-elements in order to make them coherent in action plans.
— A supervisory base that evaluates the proposals of each one of the component bases, modelling the experts' knowledge on analysing the proposals from the other bases, and leads the general inference process.

The whole can be structured as a blackboard system, each base proposing conclusions and the supervisory base putting together the results from each one in order to propose the hypotheses of the following one exactly as indicated in the figure.

Only the problem identification base and that of supervision are directly obtainable from the judgement of expert persons. The other three bases require modelling elements of knowledge proceeding from traditional modelling sources in an inferential format. In the following paragraphs a general building methology is proposed, with special attention being paid to the qualitative simulation step.

4. METHODOLOGY

4.1 Forecasting sub-base
By means of the use of the already classic time-series analysis techniques, it

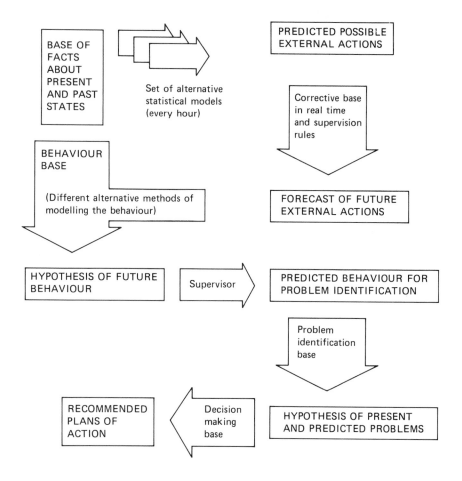

GENERAL STRUCTURE OF THE KNOWLEDGE BASE AND THE
REASONING PROCESS

is possible to formulate models that minimize the error with respect to the observed data. The use of these models in real time is not a sufficiently close approximation because of the specificity of each case. Furthermore, it is admissible for different formulation hypotheses (exponential, logarithmic, polynomial or mixed) to be adjusted in such a way that, even though one may have less expected error than another, various possible alternatives are reasonably applicable to each case.

The cognitive model to be installed can be built by:

— The set of models with different formulations of expected minimum error.
— The assessment criteria of the adjustment of the predictions of the models to the recent past of the phenomenon that is being controlled by the information system.
— The criteria for defining the most adequate formulation in view of the

registered errors for prediction and with the additions that are considered pertinent in view of the trends detected in the near past.

It is, therefore, a case of making simultaneous use of theoretical models with heuristic criteria of valuation and adaptation to the concrete problem that is being treated in real time. The building of this sub-base implies the carrying out of conventional statistical work and the contribution, by means of expert opinion on a sample of cases, of heuristic correction criteria.

The line of reasoning would consist of the following stages:

— Assessment of the discrepancies between the observed and forecast past by the different theoretical models, deducing valuations and the premise of the subsequent step.
— Identification of the best approximate theoretical formulations.
— Estimation depending on the recent errors in the approximate formulations of the additive terms or factors applicable to the theoretical forecast.
— Assessment of the estimates for the following block of time with different degrees of certainty.

The processing of this knowledge unit must be done for time blocks greater than those used for decision analysis, so that in these periods a forecast is carried out for a future time block (next hour or next two hours, for instance).

4.2 Behaviour sub-base
The purpose of this base is to provide reasoning elements, starting out from the actual state of the system and the external actions forecast, whose results proceed from the previous sub-base, so as to generate hypotheses of possible future states.

The knowledge sources for building this base are:

— The theoretical mathematical models used for simulation of the system.
— The valuations of the experts with respect to the results of the models, depending on the circumstances in which they are applied.

Apparently, the base could be constructed by incorporating into a mathematical model the previous reasoning step for the definition of data and parameters of the model and a final reasoning step from the possible results of the model.

In general, this approach suffers from excessive complexity, which makes the process difficult in real time. Because of this, a movement for using the knowledge of physical systems in qualitative terms has been produced in such a way that it is possible to make conjectures on the significant aspects of the behaviour without the need of the usual complex calculations in the simulation models. In this line, the preliminary work of Hayes (1979) and the later more technical work by de Kleer and Brown (1984), Forbus (1984) and Kuipers (1985) are significant. On general lines, these methods attempt to identify, within the different categories of states of the system, when and in what form transitions can come about. They use a formulation that leads to constraints between variables with qualitative values and carry out value-searching processes consistent with the constraint conditions.

In other cases it is possible to define a more simple representation based on a set of forward or backward reasoning rules for internal behaviour and forecasts of external actions. These rules can be obtained by means of tests or automatic learning by using the sets of results generated by the simulation model: first, it is possible to generate a sample of behaviour cases described in terms of the concepts that it is wished to inter-relate and to apply to this sample rule learning techniques of the type given by Quinlan (1979) or Michalski (1983). Doing this over several time steps, it is possible to produce rules that permit characteristics of the state of the system at different moments within the scope of the pre-fixed time grid to be inferred. The construction of this knowledge base therefore also results from a mixed process of persons' judgements, application of exploration techniques and learning with models (Cuena, 1988).

The qualitative approach may be useful combined with an approximate time assignment procedure in the cases of trunk-based flow as in traffic or floodable rivers. A general method can be defined based on the two partial differential equations of flow movement (assuming the trunk to be divided into separate contiguous sections) representing:

- Continuity of flow, expressing behaviour conditions in each section necessary for the balance between entrance and exit flows and variations in state in the section.
- The dynamic balance that expresses the conditions which must be fulfilled, by the variations, in the state of each section of the trunk in order to guarantee that movement is produced in a way consistent with the assumed dynamic principles.

From both equations, numerical schemes can be formulated of an implicit type, formed by systems of linear equations in finite differences, whose variables are the increments in the state variables (density and speed in the case of traffic, flow and depth of flow in the case of rivers) in a number of sections of the trunk into which the axis is divided for analysis purposes. The coefficients of these linear equations are obtained from the initial state at the every iteration step. The classic simulation process consists of the solution of these linear equation systems, whose results allow the evaluation of the new future state from which the process can be reconsidered, in order to generate the values corresponding to the subsequent period, over many iterations.

This quantitative method, when operating in almost real time in complex situations, has as main disadvantages the tedious computation and the difficulty of estimating the numerical forecasting values for external actions. Therefore the use of a qualitative simulation process together with an approximate analysis of time assignment of the following type is particularly useful:

- Starting from the equations in finite differences, states formulated on the basis of conditions and confluences of the type outlined by de Kleer and Brown (1984) can be defined.

- By means of a constraint satisfaction technique, given an initial state and an hypothesis of the signs of the variation of input and output flows, sets of admissible variations in the state variables and in the differences in values in links can be obtained.
- From the set of acceptable values in each section, possible states can be enumerated for the whole of the trunk. The enumeration will be made consistently with the constraints, producing value combinations of the variations of the variables in each section, ordered from greater to lesser levels of inconvenience. This level is defined by the accumulation of the inconvenience indices assigned to the changes of the variables considered in the alternative. This enumeration process can be cut by suppressing the generation of options whose disadvantage level is below a threshold.
- For each alternative generated, the possible changes in state that are consistent with its values can be defined. In this way, a range of possible future situations can be generated by enumerating the states in each section of the trunk within a pre-fixed range. Depending on the number of states obtained, extensions of the whole can be considered by means of a new process-application stage for those being less contradictory until a range of predictable future configurations of a pre-fixed size is covered.
- Once a range of possible future configurations is defined, given the structural circumstances of the system being analysed, it is possible to assign to each state an estimate of the moment at which it can happen. For this, the starting-point is a forecast table of the maximum and minimum values at each access or exit in different future instants, and estimators of the wave speed in the trunk are used to infer the maximum and minimum flow values in the sections. From these values reasoning can be carried out to assign moments of occurrence of the different states qualitatively inferred.

By means of this procedure, both the need for the estimate of spatially consistent values of the variations of state and the assignment of occurrence times to future problematic states are harmonized. This process can, in any case, be improved with off-line tests with the numerical simulator, from which heuristic criteria (to add to the knowledge base) can be deduced.

4.3 Problem identification base

This knowledge base turns out to be of a more classic type since it really constitutes a cognitive model of the management valuation criteria by its responsible persons. It therefore deals with a model of interpretation not only of initial data but also of data deduced by the behaviour model for the present or future situation, and a framework with intermediate concepts that permit referring a given situation to the different valuation categories.

The assessment of the situation allows arriving at a conclusion at different levels of evidence depending on the type of problem. The example for this sub-base is the classic one of concept-attribute-value and the building method is the well-known knowledge engineering process developed with the help of management experts.

4.4 Decision base

Once the problems have been identified it is necessary to propose consistent sets of actions that presumably affect the identified problems in a positive sense; therefore reasoning must be made from the problems to the class of actions that solve them and from these classes to the most convenient consistent subset of all of them.

The elements of this type of base can range from classification rules that, as a result, produce the conjunction of attributes to be satisfied by actions through the use of a MYCIN-type inference engine to STRIPS-type action models in which each unitary action is described by means of a trio of lists of first-order formulae: precondition, add list, and delete list of world characteristics that produce the execution of the action. With this knowledge model the inference engine must be a planner. Mixed-type architectures with classifying components connected to planning elements are admissible given the features of the case being studied. A 100% planning structure suffers from the difficulty of defining with precision the effects of the actions.

The building of this knowledge base is another case of the mixed procedure based on the criteria of expert persons and tests with models. In fact, although for the different situations an expert person is able to identify the types of action to be taken, it is not easy for him to identify in what measure they should be combined; therefore an exploration is required with a simulation model that aids in fixing these measures. In general, this research must be centred on the identification of the effects of single actions and their way of combination so that, as a result of the tests, the categories of actions are defined for the purpose of reasoning by classification or the action models for the handling of knowledge about planning.

4.5 Supervision base

The knowledge available in the different bases constitutes a premise for the next ones in the reasoning order. It is possible for the conclusions of each base not to be very clear-cut, in the sense that a series of options with different degrees of certainty may be considered possible.

Chaining between the results of one base and another cannot be established by a simple combination of degrees of certainty since the nature of the declarations of the two bases can be different; therefore, apart from chaining degrees of certainty, the conclusions of each base to be used subsequently must be supervised qualitatively with two objectives:

— Suppression of some deduced options provided that they are included in others (for example, if results have been obtained through several methods, a level of adequacy can be deduced by the supervisory base, reasoning from the case studied and the results obtained).

— Selection in order of interest and pertinence and not only in order of degree of certainty. Thus, for example, if the identification is made, although without much certainty, that an important trend can appear with a significant level representing a qualitative change (for example, an overflow, a road interruption that isolates a town, etc.) and for that reason can have effect on the decisions, it is possible to take account of this trend in advance.

— Control of the combinatorial explosion on connecting results from all bases by restricting some combinations (for example, a not very probable and unfavourable hypothesis with an excessively pessimistic simulation option).

The knowledge of this base represents the attitude of the experts not only faced with decision problems to be tolerated but also faced with the uncertainties both of the information and of the methods of behaviour representation of the system that is being studied. It will not be a very large base but, owing to its condition of meta-knowledge, its content is of great importance for the effectiveness and efficiency of the system to be developed. The methodology applicable to its construction will be the classic one of knowledge engineering using as sources expert persons in the global modelling of the system.

5.   APPLICATIONS

In the preceding paragraphs an attempt has been made to give character to a class of knowledge-based systems in which, in an operative form, the classic modelling concepts and those of artificial intelligence run side by side. Although the ideas sketched in can be consolidated in very different ways according to the problem to be resolved, the established structure is a vehicle for arranging not only the design criteria of the software to be developed but also the process of knowledge engineering.

The author of this chapter, as a consequence of his reflections, is applying a scheme of this type to the building of two knowledge-based systems to aid in decision-making in almost real time: one for the control of urban-access motorways and the other for flooding problems. The previous concepts are illustrated below, referring in a general way to the sources and type of knowledge that make up each base.

5.1   Urban-access traffic control

The purpose of the system, starting from the information on traffic (speed, density, flow) registered by sensors in real time in access motorways to important cities (Madrid, Barcelona), is to make forecasts on the future development of the quality of service and, acting on the control elements (green phases in accesses, speeds recommended inside the motorway, reversible lanes), to make recommendations to solve or improve the problems identified.

In order to meet these goals, the system has 4 components of the type already described, whose general content is described below:

5.1.1 The prediction base
The knowledge elements of this base are the forecasting models of vehicle flow to the motorway accesses together with problem-evaluation criteria and control policy. In principle, flows to the accesses are correlated among themselves so that the models correspond to a pluridimensional phenomenon, for whose adjustment it is first necessary to identify principal component series and to adjust autoregressive models to each one of them. For this adjustment Box-Jenkins-type techniques are applied first.

5.1.2 The behaviour base
The knowledge for this base will be made up of a simplified version of the flow simulation models, for which two approaches exist:

- Discrete modelling in which a file of vehicles is used and the flow behaviour results from the synthesis of the behaviours of each vehicle.
- Continuous modelling in which the magnitudes of flow measure (flow, speed, density) are handled and equations are established among them, representative of the sum-total behaviour.

Given the flow volume to be considered, discrete modelling would be impossible for handling the whole motorway; however, this type of model can be useful for refining continuous simulation models, in the area of influence of the singular points (accesses or exits). The following choices are used here:

— Discrete models for the treatment of accesses and exists.
— Continuous models for the whole of the motorway and accesses, the parameters of these models being calibrated by using the preceding models.

The continuous model is based on the equations that govern the traffic on a motorway lane j (Michalopoulos $et\ al.$, 1984): The continuity equation is

$$d_j \frac{\delta u_j}{\delta x} + u_j \frac{\delta d_j}{\delta x} + \frac{\delta d_j}{\delta t} = Q_j(x, t)$$

and the dynamic equation is

$$\frac{\delta u_j}{\delta t} + u_j \frac{\delta u_j}{\delta x} + \frac{b}{d_j} \frac{\delta d_j}{\delta x} = \frac{u_e - u_j}{C}$$

where $u_j(x, t)$, $d_j(x, t)$ are the speed and density in lane j with abscissa x along the motorway axis at moment t; u_e is a function of the density and the speed shown on control panels, which evaluate the speed desired by the drivers from these conditions.

The equations are formulated in finite-difference terms as

$$\frac{\Delta x_i}{\Delta t} \frac{\Delta d_i^j + \Delta d_{i+1}^j}{2} + um_i^j \left(\Delta d_{i+1}^j - \Delta d_i^j\right) + dm_i^j \left(\Delta u_{i+1}^j - \Delta u_i^j\right) = \Delta f_i^j$$

$$\frac{b}{dm_i^j}\left(\Delta d_{i+1}^j - \Delta d_i^j\right) + \frac{\Delta x_i}{\Delta t} \frac{\Delta u_{i+1}^j + \Delta u_i^j}{2} + um^j \left(\Delta u_{i+1}^j - \Delta u_i^j\right) = \Delta d_i^j$$

where Δd_i^j are increments in density and speed in section i lane j to be produced between t and $t + \Delta t$, um_i^j and dm_i^j are average speed and density values at moment t on the link i, lane j, Δx_i is the length of the link between sections $i, i+1$, Δf_i^j is the net access flow in lane j link $i, i+1$, in t proceeding from lateral accesses and adjacent lanes, and Δd_i^j is the dynamic imbalance in t, in the stretch $i, i+1$, lane j. It is evaluated by the balance of three terms representing (1) the imbalance between desired speed and real speed on the stretch, (2) density imbalance and (3) the speed imbalance. A rule-based version of this model could be built based on a set of significant runs of this numerical integration model (Cuena, 1988).

A qualitative simulation model based on confluences can be obtained directly from the equations in finite differences with the definitions:

- A discrete range of values of the variables of state is considered (density, speed and flow) taken from the US highway manual, grouping the first three service levels.

Service level	Density (veh/km)	Speed (km/h)	Flow (veh/h)
N	< 18	> 75	< 1000
D	18–25	65–75	1000–1200
E	25–40	50–65	1200–1600
F	> 40	< 50	> 1600

- For the variations of value of the variables the domain $(-, 0, +)$ is considered.
- As the coefficients of the equations in finite differences are always positive, the following confluences can be formulated:
  — Continuity confluence:

$$\delta dm_i^j + \delta vd_i^j + \delta vu_i^j = \Delta f_i^j \text{ where } dm_i = \tfrac{1}{2}(d_i + d_{i+1}) \tag{1}$$

  — Dynamic confluence:

$$\delta vd_i^j + \delta um_i^j + \delta vu_i^j = \Delta d_i^j \text{ where } um_i = \tfrac{1}{2}(u_i + u_{i+1}) \tag{2}$$

with the definition confluences:

$$\delta d_{i+1}^j - \delta d_i^j = \delta vd_i^j \text{ (vd}_i\text{: density variation in link } i) \tag{3}$$

$$\delta u_{i+1}^j - \delta u_i^j = \delta vu_i^j \text{ (vu}_i\text{: speed variation in link } i) \tag{4}$$

Apart from these confluences the following can be formulated:

— The confluences corresponding to the conditions at the head and tail of the trunk. For example the imposed flow condition can be represented by: $\delta d + \delta u = 0$ (formula obtained from $\delta(u.d) = 0$).
— The restrictions in the set of possible values of δu, δd due to the continuity hypothesis since, for each variable x, if the variation in the previous interval δax is known, the possible values of δx are defined by the following table:

δax	δx
$+$	$0, +$
0	$-, 0, +$
$-$	$0, -$

The inference process would be:

- Interpretation of the values of the initial state variables proceeding from the information system in the previously-described discrete domain.
- Loop
  — For each lane
    — Evaluation of Δf_i^j in each link, the forecast entry flows from outside and the rules for definition of the flow between lanes.
    — Evaluation of De_i^j using versions in rule form between discrete values of the functional formulae that appear in their expression in finite differences. This rules version can be obtained through an IDS type of learning processes (Quinlan, 1979) from samples.
    — Application of a Waltz (Winston, 1984) type of constraint satisfaction algorithm, considering the trunk sections as edges. Given the linear structure of the trunk the process is structured by solving the confluences of each link from the origin forwards, and between one link and the previous one a consistency analysis is carried out whose changes are distributed backwards.
- For each alternative, define the state transitions consistent with the signs of δd, δu, δvd and δvu. These last two values allow the definition of a partial order among the variations of the same sign since, for example, if $\delta vd_1 = +$, $\delta vd_2 = +$ and $\delta d_1 = +$, $\delta d_1 = +$ it can be stated that $\delta d_3 > \delta d_2 > \delta d_1$.
  Based on this it is assumed that the first change will happen in d_3.
- This identification of preferential changes can bring about the reduction in the number of possible next states, since several distinct alternatives of variation in values of the variables can have the same set of preferential changes, which would give rise in all of them to the same subsequent state given that the initial state is the same.
- Enumeration of transition hypotheses formed by consistent values of δd, δu in each section, ordered by level of inconvenience and above a prefixed threshold, depending on the initial state.

— The level of inconvenience of a state is estimated by the sum obtained by accumulating 1 for each occurrence of service level E and 2 for each occurrence of F. The level of inconvenience of a transition is estimated by accumulating -1 for each occurrence $\delta d_j = +$ and $\delta u_j = -$ and $+1$ for each occurrence $\delta d_j = -$ and $\delta u_j = +$.

— If the initial state already has a significant level of inconvenience above a state evaluation threshold pre-fixed as unimportant, a negative threshold for the transitions can be accepted.

These criteria express the fact that only the set of possible state transitions relevant for control purposes is required; it is superfluous to generate any other states.

As a consequence of this process, a set of possible future states are identified in order of greater to lesser inconvenience level above the indifference threshold.

The states obtained are those immediate to the initial state which are consistent with continuity and trunk flow dynamic balance conditions; however, the moment when they can be produced has not been fixed. For the purpose of decision-making, it is necessary to evaluate approximately the moment in which service levels with conflicting evaluation (E, F) can come about.

This is done by selecting, in all possible successive states, the sections in which it is forecast that this service level will appear. Once a time has been assigned, the system will warn of the possibility that this problematic service level will arise in the different sections.

The process of assigning time is carried out in the following way:

● From the analysis of time series of flows at the accesses to the freeway it is possible to define two tables at every access or exit: min_{ij} (minimum number of vehicles estimated at instant j in access i), max_{ij} (maximum number of veh/h estimated at instant j in access i) and t_{ij}, time value at instant t (the origin is the present time).

● From the analysis of the state of speeds on the freeway a travel time can be estimated for every access-section couple:

$$t_{1,i} = \sum_{k=1, i=1} \frac{\Delta x_k}{um_k} \delta k$$

where Δx_k is the length of the $k, k+1$ link and um_k is the average speed on link k, and δk is a factor for modelling the storage effect of the link with value greater or equal to 1.

● if there are no outflows between 1 and i the traffic-flow limits defined for every access 1 will arrive at every section i at the moment $t_{ij} + t_{li}$. If there are outflows it is easy to take account of these in such a way that they can be estimated for every section by interpolation in the transmitted values between a minimum (Smin) and maximum (Smax) flow at a section i at pre-fixed future instants j.

● Given a possible new state (with values in (N, D, E, F)) in a section with limits MF (minimum) and XF (maximum) (obtained as averages of the limits of the discrete states for every lane), the assignment of the time limit can be made by the criteria: (1) if MF > Smax for every predicted moment j the state is not predicatble in the near future; (2) in other cases an interval of occurrence (tmin, tmax) can be established by analysis of the couples (Smin, Smax) of the different future instants.

- The outlined reasoning allows the definition of the time interval for every future problematic state of occurrence. If a transition in a section is not acceptable for timing reasons, the section remains at the previous state.

Applications of factors for adjustment and additional heuristic criteria can be obtained from the comparison of the proposals of this model and the results obtained by quantitative simulation.

5.1.3 The problem identification base
This will be formed as has already been indicated, by a set of assessment and traffic control criteria based on the feasible problematic situations in lane sections inferred by the model; it will be constructed by classic knowledge engineering.

5.1.4 The decision base
The actions to be taken in the management of the motorway are:

- Timing green and red phases for the lights on the accesses.
- Speed recommendations in control panels.
- Reversible-lane or alternative-path recommendation.

The reasoning for these decisions can be arranged on two levels:

- Level of global analysis of the traffic situation that permits deciding whether the problems can be solved by controlling accesses locally, therefore generating additional queues, or whether it is necessary to turn to bypass or reversible channel solutions.
- Level of local decisions analysis on accesses; in this case, given that the variables to be decided take discrete values (times for green or red phases, level of recommended speed) it is possible to establish a process of classificatory reasoning that proposes the most convenient decisions in each access.

5.2 System for aiding decision-making during floods
This system, starting from real-time information on rain and water levels of a river basin, has as its objective the making of forecasts about problems of evolution and proposals for technical control and civil-defense actions (Cuena, 1983). Its general characteristics are described in the following.

5.2.1 Forecast base
In this case the external actions are the rains having an effect on the basin, whose rapid development in time gives rise to the production of floods. It is

therefore a question, as in the case of the previous section, of modelling correlated time series for which a technique can be applied of first breaking them down into principal component series and, to each one of these, applying a time series analysis.

The assessment and correction components can be defined from the analysis of observed values with respect to the adjusted models in a way similar to that established for the traffic system. In this case, the behaviour is formed by the conjunction of several phenomena:

— Surface runoff in individualized, homogeneous watersheds: the rain, on falling to the ground, is lost in part by soil infiltration while the other part remains in excess on the surface, producing a drained volume whose distribution depends on the morphology of the watershed and on its physical characteristics (vegetation and soil type).
— Rapid transport in the steepest zones. The volume drained by the watersheds passes into the network of torrents and ravines having steep slopes, in which a rapid water flow is produced, draining into the lower river courses in which the flow is produced more slowly owing to the lesser slope there.
— Final floodable river plain. In this part backwaters and canting are produced that can given rise to lateral overflows but in spite of this the main direction of flow is along the river.

A qualitative-constraint-based or rule-based model of behaviour can be defined based on the equations of unsteady flow due to Saint-Venant (Chow *et al.*, 1987).

• Continuity equation:

$$\frac{\delta Q}{\delta x} + T \frac{\delta y}{\delta t} = q$$

• Dynamic balance equation:

$$2V \frac{\partial Q}{\partial x} + \frac{\partial Q}{\partial t} + (gA - V^2 T) \frac{\partial y}{\partial x} = V^2 \frac{\partial A}{\partial x} \Big|_y + gA (S_0 - S_t)$$

where $Q(x,t)$, $V(x,t)$, $A(x,t)$, $y(x,t)$ respectively indicate volume, speed, wet area and depth of flow in t in the section whose abscissa according to the axis is x. Also, $Q(x,t) - vA$, $T(x,t)$ is the width of the free layer in section x, S_0 is the geometric gradient,

$$Sf = \frac{n^2 \, v^2}{R^{4/3}}$$

where n is the roughness coefficient and R is the hydraulic radius,

$$\frac{\partial A}{\partial x} \Big|_y$$

is the derivative of the section along the axis for constant depth (it is, therefore, null in perfectly prismatic courses), and $q(x,t)$ is the external volume for length unit x.

By using a process similar to that of section 5.1 it is possible to formulate a numerical scheme and a subsequent set of confluences for every section (the numerical scheme may be used to verify the qualitative model). This involves constructing difference equations in place of the equations of continuity and dynamic balance, above.

- Continuity confluence

$$\delta vQ_j + \delta ym_j = \Delta q \quad (ym_j = (y_j + y_{j+1})/2)$$

where Δq is the balance of accesses into the link $_j$ with values in $(-, 0, +)$.

- Dynamic balance confluence:

$$\delta vQ_i + \delta vy_i + \delta Q_{i+1} = \delta y_{i+1} + \delta y_i + \Delta d_i \tag{5}$$

as well as the definition confluences

$$\delta y_{i+1} - \delta y_i = \delta vy_i \tag{6}$$

$$\delta Q_{i+1} - \delta Q_i = \delta vQ_i \tag{7}$$

$$\delta y_{i+1} + \delta y_i = \delta ym_i \tag{8}$$

In a way similar to the case of the motorway, a process of constraint satisfaction can be established that, starting from an access hypothesis, generates sets of values of the variations of the volume and displacement variables.

Entries to the river are produced as a result of knowledge units that represent the behaviour of the basin receiving the rain in such a way that it is possible, based on a rain forecast, to define in the immediate future pairs of minimum and maximum values of the entrance volumes into the river channel.

Exits from the river are produced from the overflow states in sections; an inference step has to be taken to estimate the minimum and maximum values.

Starting from the speed state in the river, a wave velocity can be identified on which to carry out estimates of maximum and minimum volume values in each section and, by means of inference rules, to assign moments of occurrence of the different future problematic situations.

The possible states in a section can be evaluated in a discrete range of values (normal, critical, overflow) with which can be associated levels and flows in a way similar to that in section 5.1.

5.2.2 Problem-identification and decision-making bases

These two bases are both of a classical type modelling the definition of each problem, whose premisses are the levels of water. Their dynamism implies another whose content is the definition of the aspects that characterize each problem. In this sense, works on flood problem definitions in the Jucar river in Spain have already been developed whose number is around 100. Both the characterization of the problems and the actions to be taken by Civil Defence will be obtained through interviews with the responsible persons.

Control actions are basically the opening and closing of flood-gates in spillways and bottoms of dams and, therefore, a knowledge base can be constructed on the effects of accumulation of opening and closing actions defined within a discrete range of values, simulating the different possible actions with quantitative models and synthesizing the results in a decision knowledge base.

6. FINAL COMMENTS

The general description and the illustrative applications in section 5 show the feasibility of a class of knowledge-based systems that in a certain way synthesize two approaches: operations research and artificial intelligence. The construction of this type of system demands the creation of specific environments in a certain way outside of classic schemes, although derived from them, that incorporate:

— Specific inference engines for the type of reasoning applied.
— Aid to development environments that include both learning techniques and model-adjustment statistical techniques, and incorporate a formal description of the knowledge base (predefined format of rules) about the theoretical aspects.

Furthermore, in each case a conventional model system must be built previously to allow the experimental construction of any one of the knowledge sub-base components.

Systems of this type cannot *sensu stricto* be called expert since the knowledge they incorporate is not a model of a person's form of understanding but a hybrid composed of human experience of different sources and artificial empiricism generated by models. This class of systems, therefore, represents a knowledge-integration concept that can be of great utility in the field of engineering, in which at the present time there is a large stock of instrumented procedures that can serve as basis for this class of applications.

REFERENCES

Chow, V. T., Maidment, D., and Mays, L. (1987) *Applied Hydrology*, McGraw-Hill, New York.
Cuena, J. (1983) The use of simulation models and human advice to build an expert system for the defense and control of river flood. *Proc. International Joint Conference on Artificial Intelligence (IJCAI 83), Karlsruhe.*

Cuena, J. (1988) Building expert systems from simulation models: an essay on metholodogy. In M. Coombs and L. Bolc (eds.), *Computer Expert Systems,* Springer Verlag.

De Kleer J. and Brown, J. S. (1984) A qualitative physics based on confluences. *Artificial Intelligence* **24.**

Forbus, K. D. (1984) Qualitative process theory. *Artificial Intelligence* **24.**

Hayes, P. J. (1979) The naive physics manifesto. In: D. Michie (ed), *Expert Systems in the Micro-electronic Age,* Edinburgh University Press, Edinburgh.

Kuipers, B. (1985) The limits of qualitative simulation. *Proc. IJCAI-85,* W. Kaufmann, Los Angeles.

Michalopoulos, P. G., Beskos, D. E., and Yamauchi, Y. (1984) Multilane traffic flow dynamics: some macroscopic considerations. *Transport Research Board,* Vol. 18B pp. 377–395.

Michalski, R. (1983) Unifying principles and a methodology of inductive learning. *Artificial Intelligence.*

Payne, H. J. (1971) Models of freeway traffic and control. *Mathematics of Public Systems,* **1,** 51–61.

Quinlan, J. R. (1979) Discovering rules from large collection of examples: a case study. In: *Expert Systems in the Micro-Electronic Age,* Edinburgh University Press, Edinburgh.

Winston, P. H. (1984) *Artificial Intelligence,* 2nd edn. Addison-Wesley.

6

Using expert system techniques to investigate medical judgement and decision-making

G. M. van Wonderen,† C. E. Polak,‡ F. S. A. M. van Dam
University of Amsterdam, Psychological Laboratory,
Weesperplein 8, 1018 XA Amsterdam, The Netherlands

1. INTRODUCTION

Research in medical decision-making concentrates on the construction of prescriptive models which state 'how a physician should decide'. In addition it is useful to make descriptive research into medical judgement and decision making. From the point of view of patient care it is important to get a clear insight into how medical decisions are actually made. Our approach can be contrasted with the so-called statistical approach for research in medical decision-making. Advocates of the latter emphasize that decisions should be made on the explicit quantitative basis of expected results. Although the statistical approach is important and desirable there are a number of problems. The main problem is to assess precise values of possible outcomes. An additional problem is the application of the developed decision formalism in the case of an individual patient with a specific combination of medical, social and psychological problems. Moreover, Elstein (1976) argues that 'experienced, competent practitioners . . . may well know more than formal theories encompass' and advocates studying the decision making behaviour of physicians in more phenomenological terms.

We wanted to describe the complex problem of deciding about the treatment of patients suffering from an incurable disease. We were specifically interested to see whether the description would reveal the role of non-medical factors in this decision process. So the description had to include the implicit and intuitive knowledge the physician has and uses. Such a description should be dynamic and testable; just an enumeration of the factors possibly involved would not be enough. Our approach entailed the descrip-

---

† Current and correspondence address: Department of Computer Science FVI, Kruislaan 409, 1098 SJ Amsterdam, The Netherlands.
‡ Current address: Antoni van Leeuwenhoekhuis, Plesmanlaan 121, 1066 CX Amsterdam, The Netherlands.

tion of the decision process in such a way that any non-expert would be able to apply it in a specific case with the same results. We chose to make a cognitive model of the decision process of an expert concerning the choice of treatment of patients suffering from oesophageal cancer. Because the process can be complex and the number of variables large it is convenient to run the model on a computer. We found support for our ideas with Kassirer *et al.* (1982). They propose among other things to work on a cognitive theory of clinical reasoning; to investigate elements of the reasoning processes and the way they interact. This theory should be worked out in a computer program with which decision behaviour of physicians could be simulated and tested.

On the subject of human problem-solving several investigators (from various paradigms) conclude that human problem-solving is strongly dependent on domain knowledge: 'During the last decade cognitive scientists have investigated the reasoning strategies, inference engines, and representations associated with different domains of knowledge. Taken together, these studies support the general claim that inference mechanisms vary among knowledge domains. Domain-independent inference engines are doomed to failure as psychological plausible models' (Greasser and Clark, 1985). It is likely that medical expertise mainly consists of specific medical knowledge of a certain domain instead of a special good use of general problem-solving techniques (Elstein *et al.*, 1978; Kassirer *et al.*, van der Zouwe, 1983). So if we are interested in modelling a specific decision process we are mainly interested in the domain knowledge which is used. We used an Emycin-like rule language and inference engine just as a convenient formalism. We emphasize that we do not regard the inference engine as a valid model of human thinking in general.

2.   THE DOMAIN: OESOPHAGEAL CANCER

Patients sufering from cancer of the oesophagus have a cancerous growth in their gullet. With most of the patients the main complaint is the fact that they are unable to swallow solid or liquid food and drinks. In general, with swallowing and the food passage disturbances (obstruction) arise gradually. As a consequence of the obstruction in the oesophagus some patients cannot swallow their saliva; the patient constantly suffers from regurgitation and saliva might get into the bronchial tubes causing severe coughing fits, a feeling of tightness and eventually pneumonia (Gillespie and Thomson, 1977). Other symptoms are pain, chronic cough, hoarseness, swellings in the neck, hiccoughs and nausea. The problems with eating and drinking have consequences for the social life of the patient (Hoff and Zeggen, 1983).

The prognosis of this form of cancer is very bad. Fifty per cent of the patients die within six months after the diagnosis. A surgical intervention seems to be the only chance of cure. With surgery the affected sections of the oesophagus are removed if this turns out to be possible during the surgery. Some surgeons seem to be more unwilling than others to let patients undergo this possibly useless and risky operation (Polak, 1986). The aim of a palliative treatment is to make the so-called quality of life as good as possible (van Dam *et al.*, 1984; Aaronson and Calais de Silva, in press). Which one out of the possible palliative treatments would provide the best quality of life seems unclear in view of the fact that the literature reflects different opinions (Polak, 1986). The choice of a palliative treatment may be difficult for instance when one treatment could lengthen time of life whilst another might provide a better quality of life.

3.   THE CONSTRUCTION OF THE MODEL

Table 1 shows the structure of the knowledge acquisition.

Table 1

Phase	Result	By
literature	first orientation meaning of terms	studying literature
case analyses	concepts–attributes initial questions considerations	analysing patient records
interviews	relations structure of concepts heuristics support knowledge procedural knowledge	gathering data: questioning expert introspection analysing data
questionnaire surgery	checked rules indications of certainty	expert filling in while thinking aloud
questionnaire palliation	checked rules indications of certainty	expert filling in
first testing	refinement of rules	expert working with system
second testing	refinement of rules	comparing expert with system
	indication whether conclusions and line of reasoning comparable	comparing expert with system

3.1   Case analyses

We started with the study of case histories of deceased patients who were treated in the hospital in 1983. In this sort of case history all information concerning the patient is kept. The purpose was to gather concepts, expressions and notions used in order to become familiar with the domain of the expert participating in our research and to formulate initial questions. From every case we collected a list of expressions; after a review we formulated a list with more abstracted notions: concepts, attributes and relations. We also took notice of considerations mentioned in the cases concerning choice of treatment. The result was a list with about 180 classified terms, a list with possible considerations for treatment and a list of initial questions for the expert.

3.2   Interviews

The aim of the interviews was to gather information about which knowledge the expert uses and to establish how that knowledge is used when making decisions concerning treatment. Breuker and Wielinga (1986) propose to use as techniques the following: focused interview, structured interviews, introspection and self report. We applied the first three. We refer to Breuker and Wielinga (1986) for a complete review of these techniques. In a 'focused interview' all important topics are covered. In a 'structured interview' a term or heuristic is taken as a starting point and is worked out. With 'introspection' the expert is asked to imagine how he or she would solve a problem. This differs from 'self report' in which case the expert is asked to give a verbal account of his or her thinking during the real carrying out of the task. In all there have been five interviews of an hour. Transcription of the interviews proved to be indispensable.

When a surgical intervention does not seem possible, the best possible palliative treatment has to be appointed. This effectively split up our model into two parts, 'surgery' and 'palliation', even though both make partial use of the same patient data and knowledge. Also in the course of the interviewing the structure of the decision process in interaction with the patient became more clear. The interviews and the successive analysis of the interviews aimed at formalizing the expert knowledge in the model of the decision process. The analysis of the interviews had especially a function in the preparation of the next interviews; the data obtained from the interviews had to be translated into a fitting description which could ultimately be modified into a rule language. This was done by the formulation of hypothetical relations, whereby we maintained as much as possible the constructs the expert used. The hypothetical relations were maintained, rejected or modified according to subsequent interviewing.

The expert has to consider very different types of data such as the results of medical tests, information given by the patient and the expert's own experiences in interaction with the patient. The expert uses also very different kinds of knowledge, for example pure medical knowledge, knowledge concerning the emotional condition of the patient and possible reactions of the patient to the diverse manners of treatment. In addition, the expert has to work with unsteady, changeable and uncertain knowledge.

During the analysis of the interviews we had some notions of the work of Clancey (1985) concerning the inference structure of heuristic classification in mind. This does not mean that it is not possible to see the whole of the decision process as a form of 'simple classification' as soon as the system is finished. We just used the ideas of data abstraction and heuristic match as an aid to analyse the data. As well as factual or definitional knowledge we noticed that the expert used heuristic knowledge (Clancey, 1985). The following simple example will illustrate this. The expert seemed to use the heuristic 'If the tumour is large then it is probably useless to perform surgery'. We see that intermediate reasoning is implicit. The first intermediate step is also a heuristic: 'If a tumour is big then there are probable metastases'. The second step is the fact: 'if metastatic spread is present a surgical intervention is useless'. When choosing between which pieces of knowledge to represent questions arise such as:

— is the size of the tumour always known?
— is it possible that metastases are present when the tumour is small?
— according to the former verbatim reports of the expert: one seems to investigate metastatic spread although the size of the tumour is known.

The expert uses 'large tumour' which can be interpreted as a form of qualitative abstraction. So additional work concerning this piece of knowledge was to find out, for example,

— which sizes are seen as large?
— what if the tumour is somewhat smaller?
— does the expert think categorically in relating the size with treatment; if so, which categories and which relations?
— is the notion of size of the tumour clear for non-experts?

Another part of the analysis was the identification of concepts used by the expert which had to be defined further. This is essential when a user would need special expertise in order to instantiate the concept. To put it differently, whenever a user of the system would in our expectation be able to make the assessment correctly the refinement was not necessary. Our task was then to get an appropriate understanding of the meaning of these 'expert-bound' concepts. What we call an expert-bound concept is comparable with what Boose (1984) names a personal construct based on the personal-construct theory of Kelly. With questioning we then tried to make the expert express the meaning in terms of various characteristics that together form a pattern reflecting the meaning of the concept. So part of the work was to make expert-bound concepts more concrete and assessable whilst just keeping the surplus value of the expertise intact. An example is the search of the meaning of the expert-bound concept which we refer to in English as 'delicate'. The ultimate result was the decomposition of this concept into six factors which via two intermediate concepts again composes the applicability and extent of the notion concerning a specific patient. With the decomposition of 'delicate' again procedural and heuristic knowledge is involved. An additional requirement is that the certainty factor which the expert is able to associate with the original concept equals the certainty factor of the decomposed concept.

We could distinguish several types of uncertainty associated with the decision process. In order to model the decision process it is necessary to express the uncertainties. Even if the knowledge is completely modelled, the final association between data and conclusion may be uncertain, as is the case with the prediction of remaining time of life. The uncertainty could be dealt with partly via content and interactions of the rules. In other cases we applied the certainty factor model of Buchanan and Shortliffe (1984). However, a real step further would be a qualitative representation of the uncertainty.

3.3 The construction of rules

We used the structure of rules with contexts, parameters, values and certainty factors. First we tried to express complete sets of indications conclusive for a treatment in one rule. With the exception of a pattern concluding about 'chemotherapy' we stopped this appoach because we realized there were too many combinations of factors possible. Moreover, the expert did speak of an addition effect. Although it can be stated that the expert thinks about patterns, these might be constructed during the actual decision process. In our view such a pattern can be modelled by running through the system with real patient data and inspecting the built-up set of facts. So we continued with a design in which separate factors had their influence. In this context we used the certainty factor as a measure of relative importance. An objection against this approach is that the various condition parts of the rules may be not independent of each other and contribute separately to a conclusion. What could actually be seen as a separate factor we inferred from the way the expert seemed to think about it. We combined more factors in one rule when it seemed necessary. Next we tested with the questionnaires the factors about which the expert could think separately and could give an indication of importance. However, a more extensive validation is needed. An advantage of our approach is that the system builds up patterns economically.

3.4 Questionnaires

We constructed questionnaires on the basis of our developed provisional rules. The specialist could comment on form and content of the rules after an introduction into the structure of the triplet context, parameter and value. When rules were found suitable the expert could give an indication of certainty or importance associated with the rule by choosing one or more categories in a range. The expert preferred the use of qualitative categories (see example in Fig. 1).

The category 'slightly pro' stands for $(.10, .20]$ on the scale $[-1, 1]$. We used both this category and $(-.10, -.20]$ because the expert has to deal with much uncertainty on some of the factors.

The incorporation of the knowledge gathered with the questionnaires into the model developed so far led to significant changes.

3.5 The model as an expert system

The model is implemented in DELFI-2 (Lucus *et al.*, 1986), an expert system shell which has been developed at the Delft University of Techno-

If

      spread of metastases is uncertain
      the general condition of the patient is not delicate
      the estimated size of the tumour is < 7 cm

then

      the estimated life-time is . . . . > six months.

unknown | slightly pro | some indication | probably | almost surely | surely

Fig. 1.

logy. DELFI-2 is written in Pascal and runs under Unix 4.2. The inference engine works in a goal-directed way and it uses the certainty-factor model. It has convenient features such as an explanation facility, a tracing system with various options, an answer-revision system, the possibility of showing the set of established facts and some natural-language generation facilities.

The implemented model is called Oestreat. It has a rule base of 96 rules. The goal of a consultation of Oestreat is to get a treatment advice on behalf of a patient with oesophageal cancer. Put differently, the system predicts which treatments are recommended and which are not by the expert concerning a present-case patient. One can consult the system about the possibility of surgical intervention alone, which palliative treatments are preferred or both. If one consults the system about surgery and goes on with a consultation about palliative treatment, the information which is assessed during the surgery consultation is used when necessary in the line of reasoning. The beginning of a consultation by a physician is given in Fig. 2.

Figure 3 shows the conclusions of the system after this consultation was finished.

Tygontube, dilatation and laser are possible palliative treatments. The placement of a tygontube has the highest recommendations. Radiotherapy can be rejected with almost complete certainty for this patient. If a form of treatment is not mentioned in the output of the system this means that the system could not conclude anything useful concerning this treatment. For instance, if the patient has no pain, pain medication is not considered. The 'applied rule(s)' are those rules which succeeded and have a treatment in their conclusion part. So these are not all the rules which succeeded. We call the condition parts of these applied rules with a treatment in their conclusion the 'direct arguments' of the system with regard to its conclusions. The rules can be listed to inspect their condition parts. We can find the certainty factor associated with the facts in the built-up set of facts. Following the 'applied rules' mentioned by the system we consider the following elements the 'direct arguments' with regard to the conclusions given above:

— the tumour is a local recurrence (1.00 asked)
— an earlier treatment was radiotherapy (1.00 asked)
— the passage problem of the patient is serious (0.90 concluded)
— spread of metastases is sure (1.00 concluded)

Do you want some information on use?
>> n
= no (1.00)

Do you want advice on surgery?
>> n
= no (1.00)

Do you want advice on palliation?
>> y
= yes (1.00)

Is the tumour an adenocarcinoma of the distal esophagus?
>> y
= yes (1.00)

What is the age of the patient?
>> 80

Is there an esophageal fistula?
>> n
= no (1.00)

Fig. 2.

Concluded: palliative form of the treatment is:

1. tygontube, with certainty: 0.98
2. dilatation, with certainty: 0.85
3. radiotherapy, with certainty: −0.98
4. laser, with certainty: 0.88

Applied rule(s): 50, 54, 55, 56, 60, 64, 70

Fig. 3.

— the patient has not complained of pain (1.00 asked)
— the perspective (life-time) is less-six-months-more-six-weeks
   (0.65 concluded)

This way it is possible to test the system by comparing the conclusion, direct arguments and tracing chain, with the opinion of the expert about the various treatments, her arguments and her line of reasoning (thinking aloud).

During a first test of the system the expert and a colleague worked for a hour with it. The physicians noticed facts such as the absence of an important contra-indication for a surgical intervention and that during recent months the treatment with a laser had become less experimental. The expert and her colleague had no problems interacting with the system. When expert and system did not match this could easily be tracked down and explained.

3.6   Testing of the implemented model

As a second test the two physicians used four monthly-chosen patient cases. We spoke extensively about conclusions and 'reasoning of the system'. The physicians answered the questions of the system and considered to what extent the advice of the system and the justifications of it matched their own.

Table 2 shows an overview of the results; 'correct' means a fitting conclusion and 'wrong' an inappropriate conclusion compared with the actual decision of the expert.

Table 2

Consulted	Concerning	Result indicated possibilities
patient 1	surgery	correct
	palliation	wrong for radiation; correct for dilatation, laser tygontube; correct for no consideration of abstination, pain medication, chemotherapy, local radiotherapy
patient 2	palliation	wrong for radiation; correct for dilatation, laser and tygontube; correct for no consideration of abstination, pain medication, chemotherapy, local radiotherapy
patient 3	surgery	correct
patient 4	palliation	correct for dilatation, laser, tygontube, radiation; correct for no consideration of abstination, pain medication, chemotherapy, local radiotherapy

When taking the palliative treatment with the most positive certainty factor as the predicted one the results are as shown in Table 3.

With the systematic comparison the faults could be explained by some missing knowledge. Because this test is also a step in a development process we are able to improve the system with such results (which is in this case the addition of two rules and two or-conditions). Of course such testing is needed many times in order to achieve a valid cognitive model and expert system.

Table 3

Patient	Concerning	Predicted treatment	Real treatment
1	surgery	no surgery	no surgery
	palliation	tygontube	radiotherapy
2	palliation	dilatation	dilatation
3	surgery	surgery	surgery
4	palliation	tygontube	tygontube

4.   USING THE MODEL AS A RESEARCH INSTRUMENT

The goal of the development of the cognitive model was to investigate the utility of such a model as an aid in descriptive research in medical decision making. One application may be comparative research. The idea is to let various physicians decide about treatment(s) of various patients. The conclusions, the direct arguments and the line of reasoning can be compared with those of the model. If conclusions do not match we can try to formulate hypotheses describing these difference(s) in terms of the model (by deleting, adding or changing rules). We may refine and find support for these hypotheses by comparing conclusions and the line of reasoning of the adapted system and the physician on successive cases. On this level the gathered information can also be important for patients. Hereafter the research may be extended to an attempt to formulate an explanation for the differences found. Then the research aims at both a deeper representation of the knowledge and the addition of a metalevel of reasoning. The physicians may in fact have the same opinions. An example may be that when physicians seem to differ in their argumentation concerning surgical interventions they work in different hospitals with different surgery facilities, etc.

In a pilot study the model was compared with three physicians (a surgeon, an internist and a resident internal medicine specialist) involved in the choice of treatment of patients with an oesophageal carcinoma. The physicians were asked to think aloud about three patient descriptions. Two descriptions were based on real patient information. A third case only mentioned that the patient suffered from an 'oesophageal carcinoma'. These interviews were analysed in terms of the model, making it possible to hypothesize the differences between the decision processes on the level of the model.

5.   CONCLUSION

We constructed a system that models the reasoning of an expert in order to assess the best possible treatment of a patient with oesophageal cancer. It seems possible to validate this system with the techniques described in this chapter. After a complete validation a model like this could be used as a research instrument. Factors involved in the decision-making are made explicit in the form of parameters and values in the implemented model. For instance we were able to formulate an overview of all the psychosocial factors that could influence the decision. It is important to keep in mind the dynamic nature of the model. The influence of a factor is only known if the model is consulted with patient data. Models like this could contribute to the formulation of a theory about medical judgement and decision making. Moreover, each such model provides a clear view of *what* kind of factors are involved in these very important decisions.

ACKNOWLEDGEMENTS

The authors wish to thank the interviewed expert and H. van Dalen.

REFERENCES

Aaronson, N. K. and Calais da Silva, F. (1987) The measurement of quality of life in cancer research. In: U. Verones, I. Burn, L. Denis, and F. Mazzeo (eds.), *European Handbook of Surgical Oncology*, Springer-Verlag, Berlin, in press.

Boose, J. H. (1984) Personal Construct Theory and the Transfer of Human Expertise, *Proceedings AAAI '84.*

Breuker, J. A. and Wielinga, B. J. (1987) Use of models in the interpretation of verbal data. In A. Kidd (ed.), *Knowledge Elicitation for Expert Systems: a Practical Handbook*, Plenum Press, New York.

Buchanan, B. G. and Shortliffe, E. H. (eds.) (1984) *Rule-Based Expert Systems: the MYCIN experiments of the Stanford Heuristic Programming Project*, Addison-Wesley, Reading, Mass.

Clancey, W. J. (1985) Heuristic classification. *Artificial Intelligence*, **27**.

van Dam, F. S. A. M., Linssen, A. G., and Couzijn, A. L. (1984) Evaluating "quality of life" in cancer clinical trials. In: M. Buyse, M. Staquet and R. Sylvester (eds.), *Cancer Clinical Trials: Methods and Practice*, Oxford University Press, London, pp. 26–43.

Day, N. E., Munoz, N., and Ghadiran, P. (1982) Epidemiology of esophageal cancer, a review. In: P. Correa and W. Haenszel (eds.), *Epidemiology of Cancer of the Digestive Tract.*

Elstein, A. S. (1976) Clinical judgement: psychological research and medical practice. *Science*, **194**, 696–700.

Elstein, A. S., Shulman, L. S., and Sprafka, S. A. (1987) *Medical Problem Solving: A Analysis of Clinical Reasoning*, Harvard University Press, Cambridge, Mass. and London, UK.

Gillespie, I. E. and Thomson, T. J. (1977) *Gastroenterology, an Integrated Course*, Churchill Livingstone, Edinburgh, London, New York.

Greasser, A. C. and Clark, L. F. (1985) *Structure and Procedures of Implicit Knowledge*, Ablex, New Jersey.

Hoff, M. and Zeggen, L. (1983) Problems of patients with a non operable oesophagus carcinoma (in Dutch), *doktoraal werkstuk*, Amsterdam.

Kassirer, J. P., Kuipers, B. J., and Gorry, G. A. (1982) Special article:

toward a theory of clinical expertise. *The American Journal of Medicine*, **73** (August), 251–259.

Lucus, P. J. F., de Swaan Arons, H., and Stienen, H. (1986) *DELFI-2 Manual* (in Dutch), TH Delft.

Polak, C. E. (1986) The oesophagus carcinoma and quality of life (in Dutch), *doctoraalscriptie*, Department of Psychology, University of Amsterdam.

Shortliffe, E. H. (1976) *Computer-based Medical Consulations: MYCIN*, Elsevier, New York.

van der Zouwe, N. (1983) Decision making and therapy indications (in Dutch), *doctoraalscriptie*, Department of Psychology, University of Amsterdam.

Part III

AI methods in design

7

Expert systems for design: basic techniques

Norberto R. Iudica
Battelle-Institut e.V., Am Römerhof 35, D-6000 Frankfurt 90, W. Germany

SUMMARY

In this chapter the design of industrial products is considered from the point of view of the knowledge-representation and processing techniques involved, in order to provide a first reference and a stimulus for starting research projects in the subject. The artificial intelligence techniques relevant for design applications are considered, and some of the most critical are chosen for a brief introduction, some observations and an outlook.

1. INTRODUCTION

This chapter tries to show how interesting artificial intelligence research subjects can be derived out of the requirements for more or less realistic knowledge-based design systems, producing practical results as a by-product. For this purpose the generalities of the industrial design process will be considered first and then those aspects where artificial intelligence could be applied will be outlined.

Industrial design is the process of producing the description of a manufacturable object which fulfils a function while satisfying a set of given constraints. Design involves, then, representation, manipulation and understanding of objects, relations, standards and scientific laws combined with creative imagination. That is, practically all fields of artificial intelligence can be applied, including natural-language understanding (for standards and requirements) and vision (for the interpretation of drawings).

It is this richness combined with the perspective of deriving intermediate results of industrial interest that is stimulating research in the field. Some recent application-oriented work includes design of photocopier subassemblies, VLSI design, and design of gearbox housings and axles.

1.1 Attempting to identify AI techniques required

By studying several case studies in real life and in the literature, it is possible to attempt to list the activities that a designer should be able to implement through the primitives provided in a knowledge-based systems building tool.

1.1.1 Multiplicity of paradigms and of knowledge sources

A designer cannot express his or her knowledge on design through any particular single paradigm. As a rule, different methods will be needed for different design problems or for different aspects of the same design. It is thus necessary to provide a selection of proven paradigms together with the possibility of creating new ones.

The knowledge for real-world design tasks will be usually distributed in different sources. There will be design rules that apply to the same object under different circumstances or under different requirements or valid standards. Design systems need great quantities of detailed knowledge; if expressed as rules, hundreds to thousands of them will be necessary for any relevant application.

1.1.2 Problem decomposition

It is always convenient to reduce a task to a set of more simple ones, be it for the early detection of dead-ends, for ease of control or for distributing the responsibility for its execution. The kind of problem decomposition needed can be for expressing a sequence of design steps or for the hierarchical decomposition of a given task.

1.1.3 Management of assumptions and alternatives

A design is not always completely specified in advance; some options are usually left open. The designer faces thus the need of assuming values for different design parameters in order to be able to start the design process or to explore different design alternatives. In some cases lacking a workable model of the design object, it may be necessary to supply a value without knowing precisely in advance how the design is going to be affected.

The data introduced for filling these gaps in the formal knowledge or in the specifications must be recorded as assumptions and the design data produced out of them are to be managed in a way that permits switching to different sets of data (a kind of alternative design) to evaluate, validate, record or reject them.

The designer must have the capability of rewinding the design to some arbitrary stage and to recommence with different assumptions, choice of components or optimization criteria. It must also be possible to explore several options in parallel or sequentially in order to sort out the most appropriate one.

1.1.4 Constraints and failures

A design problem is characterized by constraints of different kinds; some relate to the feasibility of the task in economical or in technical terms, others relate to interrelations to be observed between the components because of functionality considerations, and other constraints finally express consequences of natural laws.

The designer makes use of the constraints to reduce the spectrum of possible options at each point where a decision is to be made as well as for early detection of undesirable or infeasible results.

It is important to be able to detect basic incompatibilities, loops or dead ends that lead to a failure of the design process under the given set of data assumptions and knowledge. Once a failure has been detected some mechanism for dealing with it should be used in order to bring the system back to the correct path.

Normally a designer records the environment of a failure as well as its identified or suspected causes. The knowledge gained in this way can be used only once to guide the design process at hand, but in general the designer learns to recognize the bad situations and to avoid them from the beginning, improving his or her performance.

1.1.5   Formal qualitative knowledge and simulation

The use of knowledge about the approximate relation between physical magnitudes and some causal knowledge allows the designer to decide on the direction of change of design parameters or on which parameters are the suspected cause of wrong designs. In many design cases the available knowledge will not be enough to ensure that the designed object will perform as desired. For these sorts of situations the designer is usually in a position to simulate the function of his or her creation under some set of worst-case conditions. The simulation may be numerical, or just conceptual through a qualitative appreciation of the physics involved.

1.2   Focusing on some critical techniques

Specially relevant for the purpose of presenting techniques that need refinement and extension but have already found some practical application are:

— knowledge representation
— constraint-based reasoning
— non-monotonic reasoning

These three subjects are not only central to present research and development work in the field but are also interrelated. This is in the sense that the constraints can be represented as frames, that non-monotonic reasoning has to deal with constraints and that both non-monotonic reasoning and constraints play a central role in 'qualitative physics' systems which can in turn be used to build more intelligent non-monotonic reasoning and constraint-based systems.

2.   KNOWLEDGE REPRESENTATION

Knowledge representation means the creation, classification and storage of descriptions of objects. They can be physical objects, abstract or auxiliary objects(such as kinds of objects or status of a system) or facts, relations between facts or sequences of actions.

An object can be described by its attributes and each attribute admits properties. It is often useful to classify related objects in a taxonomic hierarchy, inventing generalized intermediate entities to represent sets of more concrete or specialized ones.

In general, not only declarative and procedural knowledge must be represented but also the high-level representation of the entities this knowledge refers to and operates upon. Basic entities for design are:

— physical objects in general
— relations between objects or attributes of objects
— rules
— tasks

2.1 Frames

At present the most practical and flexible structure for knowledge representation is the **frame**. Frames are structured descriptions of objects, consisting of a set of data structures called **slots** which contain the information corresponding to an attribute. Each slot consists of a set of **facets** describing the properties of the representation of the corresponding attribute.

A frame can be used to describe either the characteristics shared by a set of objects, called a **class**, or some concrete individual object member of a class, that is, of an **instance** of that class. Concrete objects can only be produced as instances of classes having no further subclasses; they are thus called **terminal instances**.

Classes are related to each other through hierarchical relations. Each subclass specializes its superclass by refining the description (i.e. the set of slots inherited from it) by adding more slots.

The hierarchy of classes is headed by a class called usually 'class', which is the superclass of all classes and has itself some conventional abstract class as superclass.

There are several frame systems; some are embedded in expert system building tools and others are self-contained. All the frame systems are based on the principles similar to those above; the differences between them reside mainly in the way of defining the classes and their relationships and in the details of the inheritance process.

2.2 Specializing the frames for design purposes

For applications in design systems, some additional characteristics are needed that are not usually offered by commercial tools. These extra characteristics include two new types of objects and some special facets.

In design systems, terminal instances can either be produced at run-time, as they usually are, or be compiled and always present, to represent the static parts of the problem, such as technological constraints, fixed-solution schemes and so on. These compiled terminal instances are called **fixed instances**; they are intended to be manipulated by the expert. For the end user they must behave as any other instance with the difference that they cannot be modified.

Another special kind of instance is needed for successive refinement of a partially-specified object. That can be realized through a non-terminal instance to which attributes can be assigned gradually and that can be dynamically reclassified according to the slots present and to their contents.

In addition to the standard facets normally used in general-purpose frames (i.e. those for value, type, cardinality, default and attached procedures) extra facets are needed to contain pointers to relations affecting the value of the slot; in this way constraints can be directly referred to the values they link.

2.3   Representation of objects in design systems

2.3.1   Physical objects in general

The exact format and the extension of the description of physical objects is application-dependent, but in general terms an object description should contain the following items:

- name: string that identifies the object.
- part_of: reference to another object that contains this one as a subpart.
- sub_parts: set of references to other more detailed descriptions of parts that compose the object; they allow a hierarchical representation of objects.
- nr_of_sub_parts: an integer that identifies the number of object subparts.
- relations: set of references to other frames that describe instances of relations in which the object is involved.

2.3.2   Relations between objects

Relations between objects can be represented as in the following scheme:

- name: string that identifies the relation.
- first_arg: the first entity involved in the relation.
- second_arg: the second entity involved in the relation.

Pointers to instances of relations are contained in the frame representation of the entities involved in the relation.

The use of independent frames to represent relations between objects offers several advantages: it is a flexible formalism that prevents the object representation from being redundant and allows the presence of a relation to be tested explicitly and it also makes it possible to represent relations created at run-time.

2.3.3   Rules

Production rules as normally used in knowledge-based systems are also useful for design provided that they contain a slot for actions and another for conclusions and a third one for assigning them to different partitions for different purposes.

2.3.4   Tasks

A task is the scheme of a problem to be solved; it is useful for giving problems (or subproblems) a reference name as well as for concentrating information related to its solution.

Tasks can be represented according to the following scheme:

- name: the name can contain one argument for passing arguments to the task.
- preconditions: list of facts that must hold for the task to be useful.
- responsible_for: the list of the main results expected from the execution.
- methods: list of actions that represent different alternatives for executing the task.
- postconditions are the conditions (satisfied constraints) for considering the task as successfully terminated.

3.   TRUTH MAINTENANCE

3.1   Introduction

We say that **a system reasons non-monotonically** if derived facts must be changed during the problem-solving process.

The need to update the current set of believed facts (beliefs) at run-time may be required for several reasons:

- beliefs depend on working hypotheses that turn out to be incompatible
- beliefs depend on a set of facts that lead to an undesired result
- the conditions under which problem-solving is done change (the world changes dynamically or alternatives are required)

A **truth maintenance system** (TMS) is used as a general mechanism to allow a problem solver to reason non-monotonically and to record the dependences of derived facts.

Non-monotonic reasoning requires from the problem solver the capability of appropriately revising its current set of beliefs whenever needed. Every belief must have a justification in terms of other beliefs that have been used to establish it and, if needed, also those beliefs on whose absence it relies. These justifications are used to identify the premises and assumptions a belief is based on, as well as all the beliefs depending on a particular premise or assumption.

Generally, a TMS works on behalf of a problem-solving system responsible for the overall control of the reasoning process. The current set of beliefs, together with their justifications, is stored in a dependency network. The problem-solver adopts or abandons beliefs by means of inferences or observations and justifies these beliefs by corresponding reasons. The TMS updates the current set of beliefs with respect to these modifications.

3.2   TMS after Doyle

In this approach all the inferences of a problem solver are recorded by the TMS in the form of a dependency network. This network consists of a set of nodes, representing the beliefs of a problem solver, and a set of justifications, representing the reason(s) for a belief.

The TMS can do the following operations on this dependency network:

— generating new nodes
— adding justifications to an existing node
— marking a node as a contradiction

A justification consists of two lists of nodes: in-list and out-list. It is allowed for a node to have more than one justification. Whether a node is 'in' or 'out' (i.e. whether it is believed by the problem solver or not) can be determined by examining its justification. A node is 'in' if one of its justifications is valid. A justification is valid if all the nodes in its in-list are 'in' and all the nodes in its out-list are 'out'.

The TMS has the following tasks:

• If it is supplied with a new justification for a node, it has to find a consistent in/out labelling of the nodes (through maintenance).
• If a valid justification for a node marked as a contradiction is established, it has to resolve this contradiction (dependency-directed backtracking).

Truth maintenance is essentially a constraint-satisfaction problem, that is, to find a labelling of in or out for the nodes that is consistent with the corresponding justifications.

3.3   TMS after de Kleer

In this approach, called ATMS (for **assumption-based** TMS) the inferences made by the problem solver are also recorded in the form of a dependency network, again given by a set of nodes, representing the beliefs, and a set of justifications for these beliefs.

Every node contains an additional label describing all the sets of assumptions under which the node holds. A set of assumptions is called an **environment**; a node can hold under several sets of assumptions, that is, a node label can contain multiple environments.

An environment is said to be **inconsistent** if, under the assumptions contained in it, it is possible to derive something undesirable, for instance a contradiction.

A **context** is the set formed by the assumptions of a consistent environment together with all data derived from them.

The environment of a node is a compact representation of all the contexts in which a node holds: a node holds in a context if one of its environments is contained in this context. By this technique it is possible for the problem solver to switch between different contexts (i.e. alternative solutions) at no cost.

If a contradiction is detected, the environment of the contradiction is recorded as a nogood. Every node having an environment containing a nogood is then inconsistent.

3.4 Truth maintenance as required in design systems

Truth maintenance systems along the lines of Doyle's keep at any time only one set of consistent beliefs (one 'world'); when one belief changes status all its consequences must be affected by a process called **dependency-directed backtracking** (DBB) to create a new 'world'.

ATMS in its pure, unrestricted form is usually used to work in parallel in all possible alternative 'worlds' with a mechanism called 'consumer architecture'. Once the problem is solved, it is possible to switch from one solution to the other since all of them are obtained.

Both approaches have advantages and disadvantages. DDB is easy to follow and can provide better explanations because the system is always focused in one solution space but for obtaining further solutions the system must be partially re-run. DDB is the best choice when only few solutions exist or are interesting. ATMS working with the consumer architecture is almost impossible to follow and can give no sensible tracing because it does not follow any defined line of reasoning but produces all solutions. ATMS is to be preferred if a large number of useful solutions based on different sets of data is expected and desired.

De Kleer's ATMS is able to provide an efficient way of dealing with alternatives that can be used to implement a variety of extensions and special case mechanisms based on the information available in the nodes and in the environments. For the most part these mechanisms are based on grouping together environments to form control disjunctions which can be used to communicate bi-directionally with the problem solver. In this way it is possible to force the problem-solving process to consider, to avoid or to ignore some context(s) (or worlds) and to provide DDB.

Some research subjects that can be derived from the actual state of TMS systems are related to design applications. One point is the extension of the concept of 'falsity' to include the test of results so far for consistency with a set of constraints or verification with a procedure. This is required to verify a design according to technological criteria. The actual implementations of ATMS have no explicit representation of negation and no provision for fuzzy operators. An extension in this sense would allow a more natural expression of technical knowledge. Means for permitting the problem-solver to express its interest or lack of interest in some sets of solutions must be developed for restricting the set of designs to those that are really meaningful. Finally, the results of present research on the field of qualitative physics must be investigated for their prospective use in helping problem solvers in choosing solutions or assumptions on the basis of a deeper knowledge of the phenomena involved.

4. CONSTRAINTS

4.1 Introduction

A **constraint** is a relationship between different variables. These constraints can be generated by a design system during the problem-solving process in order to state certain relationships between various design parameters.

Constraints can be used as **elimination rules** by interpreting them as conditions to be satisfied when trying to decide on values for design parameters. They can also be used as **partial descriptions** and **commitments in design refinement**; during the design process there are often many ways for deciding which part of the design is to be refined and how.

Deciding on a specific value for some part of the design might lead to contradictions later on, when other parts are refined. One way to overcome these difficulties is to state constraints instead of specific values for the design variables, where a constraint is a partial description of some design variable that can be refined in later stages of the solution process when more details are known.

Another use for constraints is as **expressions describing the interactions between subproblems**. For this purpose, a constraint describes a relationship between (possibly uninstantiated) design variables. These variables are often shared among various steps in a design. Constraints imposed by different parts of the problem can then be combined to derive new constraints, either on the same variables or on variables used in other parts of the design. By this process it is possible to bring together the requirements from different parts of the problem and to account for interactions between them.

4.2   Operation with constraints

Constraint formulation is the process of generating new constraints during the problem-solving process. The dynamic generation of constraints enables a design system to proceed hierarchically by imposing constraints of increasing detail as the solution evolves.

Constraint propagation is the process of inferring new constraints from already-existing ones. This inference allows a system to merge the requirements imposed by different parts of a design. The propagation of constraints can occur on various levels:

- Combining all the restrictions on one design variable in order to derive a refined restriction or to detect a conflict.
- Deriving new constraint expressions from existing ones.

During constraint propagation the system obtains automatically all the consequences of the change in one value that can be derived from the combination of declared constraints directly or indirectly connected with it. In a typical application when either the 'true' or the 'constrained' value for an object attribute subjected to a constraint is obtained, the constraint processing mechanisms either accept and propagate this value, or reject it, producing a 'conflict' situation.

Constraint satisfaction is the process of assigning values to the variables so that all the constraints imposed on them by the designer are satisfied. Methods for constraint satisfaction can be based on the local propagation principle where values (or restrictions on values) for the variables are propagated through a constraint net that is built up from the single constraints imposed by the system.

Conflicts occur whenever the constraint-processing mechanisms define a value in such a way that it cannot exist.

Constraint consultation can be used to provide default values for attributes of objects that are subjected to a relation with other entities. The result will be the set or interval currently believed to contain the required value and it can be used to restrict further the set of possible values, to pick one as an assumption, etc.

4.3   Constraint techniques for design systems

Constraints are not provided in commercial knowledge-based system-building tools and even in research prototypes many points are still left uncovered. In the following, some essential requirements for the best use of constraints are given.

The prepresentation of constraints should be frame-based with a well-defined and simple mechanism to relate the values of the slots involved in a relation with the representation of the relation itself, for instance through special-purpose facets. It should be possible to create constraints either off-line (for permanent relations) or at run-time (for relations determined during the design process).

The description of permanent constraints by the user must be facilitated by special editors which should recognize an expression written according to the normal technical conventions and related attributes of objects in the 'world' of the application and automatically produce all the internal representations and pointers needed. The classes of constraints supported should include boolean and arithmetic constraints providing interval calculations and comparisons as well as simplification of expressions.

Mechanisms for communicating the appearance of conflicts to an ATMS should be provided. The permanent constraints could include in themselves suggestions for the case of constraint violation as well as a qualifier to evaluate their relative importance in case of conflict with other constraints.

Finally, efficient implementations are needed, or else basing the solution of a complex problem on constraints becomes frustrating.

5.   OTHER RELEVANT PROBLEMS

Although — in order to avoid being eclectic — not further developed in this chapter, there are other matters relevant to product design with a high theoretical interest which are less mature than the three mentioned here. This is specially the case for 'qualitative physics' and for the bi-directional coupling between knowledge-based and CAD systems.

6.   CONCLUSIONS

We have seen that design, being a highly complex activity, provides an excellent research environment for different artificial intelligence techniques of general applicability. All three techniques mentioned can, for instance, be applied to fields from diagnosis to planning and process control.

While the inherent difficulty of design and its strategic importance for a corporation will avoid the full automation of design in general and for the whole process from the strategic and marketing decisions down to the production of prototypes, it will be increasingly possible to automate routine design, design of variants, configuration and rough design as needed for tendering.

There are many possibilities for applied research based on the subjects mentioned in this chapter. The possibilities range from design systems using some particular new approach or combination of techniques to the extension, adaptation or substitution of what is currently available, for example use of qualitative physics for focusing problem-solvers or for intelligent failure recovery, and of non-monotonic reasoning systems using fuzzy operators.

BIBLIOGRAPHY

The minimal list of references given below should ease the interested reader into the first step towards a deep understanding of the subjects mentioned in this article and give a source for further references.

Frames and knowledge representation
Special section on architectures for knowledge-based systems. *Communications of the ACM*, **28** (9) (September 1985).
Winston, P. H. *Artificial Intelligence*, 2nd edition, Addison-Wesley. 1984.

Truth maintenance systems
Artificial Intelligence, **28** (1986).

Constraints
Steele, G. J. and Sussman, G. L. Constraints: a language for expressing almost hierarchical descriptions. *Artificial Intelligence*, **14** (1980).
Steels, L. Constraints as consultants. In: L. Steels (ed.): *Progress in Artificial Intelligence*, Ellis Horwood Limited, Chichester 1985.

Design
Latombe, J. C. Artificial intelligence in computer aided design: the TROPIC System. In J. J. Allan (ed.): *CAD Systems*, North-Holland 1977.
Horváth, M. and Markus, A. Prototype of a Prolog-based design engine. *Proceeding of the International Symposium on Design and Synthesis, Tokyo, 1984.*
Mittal, S. and Araya, A. A knowledge-based framework for design. *Proceedings of AAAI-86.*
Mostow, J. Toward better models of the design process. *The AI Magazine* (Spring 1985)
Aquesbi, A. *et al.* An expert system for computer aided mechanical design. In: R. E. A. Mason (ed.), *Information Processing 83*, Elsevier Science Publishers.

Qualitative physics
Artificial Intelligence, **24** (1980).

8

Knowledge engineering in design

Varol Akman, Paul ten Hagen, Jan Rogier and **Paul Veerkamp**
Department of Interactive Systems, Centre for Mathematics
and Computer Science (CWI), Kruislaan 413, 1098 SJ
Amsterdam, The Netherlands

SUMMARY

We present in a unifying framework the principles of the IIICAD (intelligent, integrated, and interactive computer-aided design) system. IIICAD is a generic design apprentice currently under development at CWI. IIICAD incorporates three kinds of design knowledge. First, it has general knowledge about the stepwise nature of design based on a set-theoretic design theory. Second, it has domain-dependent knowledge belonging to the specific design areas where it may actually be used. Finally, it maintains knowledge about the previously-designed objects; this is somewhat similar to software re-use. Furthermore, IIICAD uses AI techniques in the following areas: (i) formalization of design processes, extensional vs. intensional descriptions, modal and other nonstandard logics as knowledge representation tools; (ii) commonsense reasoning about the physical world (naive physics), coupling symbolic and numerical computation; (iii) integration of object-oriented and logic programming paradigms, development of a common base language for design.

'In this paper, I have tried to argue that there is an important class of problems in knowledge representation and commonsense reasoning, involving incomplete knowledge of a problem situation, that so far have been addressed only by systems based on formal logic and deductive inference, and that, in some sense, probably can be dealt with only by systems based on logic and deduction.' (Moore, 1985).

1. INTRODUCTION

Recent research in computer-aided design (CAD) (cf. Yoshikawa and Warman (1987), Gero (1985, 1987) and ten Hagen and Tomiyama (1987) for some representative articles and Lansdown (1988) for a good, nontechnical review) has shown a visible interest in the *intellectualization* of design. We find this a healthy trend since we believe that the ultimate aim of CAD is the automation of the several knowledge-intensive activities performed today solely by highly specialized, hard to come by, expensive, and unfortunately error-prone human experts. In fact, it is not too early to claim that manufacturers are already very interested in 'intelligent CAD' since several useful research efforts have been made, e.g. Briggs and Stratton's Engineering Design Assistant (Skylar, 1987). A common view goes like this: "Right now there are several designers who know a little about all facets of engine design, but there is no individual who could effectively design an entire engine. Eventually, however, it may be possible for one person, using a collection of expert systems, to do a considerable amount of the engine design process." (Skylar, 1987).

Intelligent CAD is practised mainly by applying the already-existing ideas of artificial intelligence (AI) and knowledge engineering (KE) in several aspects of the design process/object modelling. In addition to making CAD more intelligent, this approach has the advantage that while studying the appropriate AI and KE techniques, CAD researchers contribute to the existing body of knowledge in these areas.

The need to make CAD more sophisticated is real and being felt today especially in the high-tech domains. As technologies advance, the management of the complexity as a result of the amount and variety of information to be handled by design systems is becoming a gigantic task. It is hoped that advances in AI will be a keystone in bringing promising low-term solutions to structuring this potentially explosive domain of knowledge. The weaknesses of the existing CAD systems today are basically due to the facts that (i) they have no task-domain knowledge to reflect the thinking processes, terminology, and intentions of designers, and (ii) the system software is written in an unstructured, *ad hoc*, and hard to maintain/upgrade way, with no sound basis (in terms of a formal design theory).

We see intelligent CAD as a theory resting on a triad: a theory of knowledge, a theory of design processes, and a theory of design entities (objects). Our work at CWI is aimed at contributing to these theories and evaluating their usefulness through prototype implementations treating real design problems. We should add immediately that we are not interested in 'expert systems for design' *per se* although we consider them as part of the grand picture (Bobrow *et al.*, 1986).

Clearly, the proposition that one has a 'theory' to deal with design is rather pretentious and even dangerous. We are aware of the fact that design is a 'mysterious' activity which is currently done in its entirety only by intelligent human designers. Yet, to quote Lansdown (1988):

'[I]n broad terms, most people would accept that designing is a cyclical process in which concepts are devised and then tested against some criteria of performance, cost, or appearance. The tests: logical, physical, or just intuitive, lead to the concepts either being incorporated into the design or being rejected. In any event, the testing process gives rise to the formulation of new concepts and, importantly, then to new criteria for testing. The whole of designing thus is governed by what Ernst Gombrich calls "schema and correction" — almost a trial and error process where experimentation precedes correction which in turn leads to further experimentation.'

We appreciate the difficulty of identifying and incorporating all the planning, heuristic, and inventive knowledge that good designers tend to have. (Cf. Brown and Chandrasekaran (1986), Mittal *et al.* (1986) and Dyer *et al.* (1986) for several researchers' views on the various aspects of design.) Nevertheless, the issue here is mainly that of a formal language to 'communicate' our results to the outside world. We believe that even in the vague domain of design where any kind of formalization would probably look superficial, a formal outlook is the only way to do scientific research. We see logic as the essential framework of this formal outlook. First, logic is precise and unambiguous with a well-understood semantics that connects the formulae of logic and the real world that they talk about. Second, in its purity, logic provides a high level of abstraction since it is entirely nonprocedural. It also acts as a formal specification since the knowledge is not buried in procedures. This issue is of substantial help in writing software engineered CAD code.

The organization of this chapter is as follows. In section 2, we briefly look at a logical formalization of the design processes. In Section 3, knowledge representation issues in design are reviewed from the angle of intensional vs. extensional descriptions. A theory of design entities based on naive physics and coupled systems is summarized in Section 4. Combining object-oriented and logic programming styles to arrive at a design base language is studied in Section 5. Finally Section 6 summarizes the key propositions of our approach and suggests future directions.

This chapter, because of space limitations, is only a short, partial overview of our research. The reader is referred, in addition to several other foundational articles by Tomiyama and Yoshikawa to be referenced later, to Veth (1987a–c) and Tomiyawa and ten Hagen (1987a–c) for a detailed exposition of our work.

2. A LOGICAL FORMALIZATION OF DESIGN PROCESSES

2.1 The stepwise nature of design

We use general design theory (Tomiyawa and Yoshikawa, 1987) as a basis for formalizing design processes and design knowledge. The theory is based on axiomatic set theory and models design as a mapping from the *function* space, where the specifications are described in terms of functions, onto the *attribute* space where the design solutions are described in terms of attributes. Roughly speaking, one starts with a functional specification of the design object and ends with a manufacturable description encompassing all its attributes.

The basic ideas behind a logical formalization of design processes are as follows:

- From the given functional specifications a candidate is selected and refined in a stepwise manner until the solution is reached, rather than trying to get the solution directly from the specifications.
- Hence design can be regarded as an evolutionary process which transfers the model of the design object from one state to another. We call this model, being a set of attributive descriptions, a *metamodel*. (This rather confusing and uninformative name is kept for historical reasons.)
- During the design process new attributive descriptions will be added (and some existing ones will be modified) and the metamodel will hopefully converge to the solution. Since dead-ends are natural occurrences in design, a technique to step back and select more promising paths at any time is also required.
- To evaluate the current state of the design object (i.e. the metamodel), various kinds of models of the design object need to be derived from the metamodel in order to see whether the object satisfies the specifications or not. We call those models of the design object *worlds* and they can be regarded as interpretations of the design object seen from certain points of view — the concept of 'multi-worlds'. (In machine design, one such model would be the finite-element model of the design object, for instance.)

Considering the metamodel evolution model, the system starts from the specifications, s, of the design object and continues with the design process until the goal, g, is reached. We define q_j^i as the set of propositions at the state of metamodel M^i with an interpretation in world w_j. In other words, if we have m worlds then $q_1^i, \ldots, q_m^i$ constitute the current state of knowledge about the design object. There are two possibilities: either the current state of knowledge is complete and consistent or there is an incompleteness/inconsistency. In the first case, g has been reached and we have finished the design process. In the latter case, there is a need to proceed to the next metamodel M^{i+1} in order to resolve the incompleteness or inconsistency. (Note that we do not care about the inconsistency of a *particular* world.)

The nature of design then, understood in the above sense, is to modify/add properties about the design object. This means that we need language contructs to evaluate a metamodel by creating worlds and to derive new properties or to update uncertain/unknown properties in such a world in order to get more detailed knowledge about the design object. The crucial point is how to proceed from M^i to M^{i+1}. Alternatively, we can pose the following questions. How do we define q_j^i? How do we derive new information from the current world and compare different worlds? It has to be realized that we are not aiming at an automated design environment; our system is meant to be a *designer's apprentice*. The designer should take the initiative for directing the design process. This is where the interactive nature of design comes into play. Accordingly, the designer, regarding a certain world, can modify/add attributes about the design object. The system evaluates the metamodel after these updates and checks it for consistency.

The reader may notice that it seems natural to choose modal logic as a representational language since modal logic deals with interpretations of a model (understood in the 'logical' sense) in multiple worlds (again understood in the logical sense). We do not elaborate on the relationship between the meanings we attach to 'model', 'world' and the usual interpretation of these words as employed in modal logic; cf. Hughes and Cresswell (1972) for details.

Design, at the highest level, is accomplished in IIICAD by interacting with the so-called *scenarios* which are (conceptually) frame-like structures describing standard design procedures. The classical definition of frames '. . . a data structure for representing a stereotypical situation like being in a certain kind of living room or going to a child's birthday party' (Minsky, 1975). Just like frames, scenarios have information about the design objects/ processes that play a role in stereotypical design situations as well as the various relationships between the stored information. Each scenario tells something about the way it is to be used and gives clues as to what to do if something goes wrong with the current design while it is active. The notion of default values for slots has a counterpart 'assumed' attribute values for design entities. A scenario base is then a collection of scenarios structured in terms of some organizational principles. The following principles are well-known (Mylopoulos and Levesque, 1984):

- *Classification/generalization*. One can associate a scenario with its generic type. Thus a scenario to design, e.g. a bicycle lock belongs to the generic type 'locks'. The generalization relation between types is a partial order (lattice) and structures types into an *isa-hierarchy*. An isa-hierarchy provides the means for the overall organization and management of a large scenario base. Additionally and more technically, isa-hierarchies reduce the storage requirements by allowing properties associated with general objects to be passed to more specialized ones.
- *Aggregation*. This relates a scenario to its components (parts). Aggregation can be applied recursively to represent the parts of the parts. For example, the parts of a bridge are its toll booths, supports, traffic lights, pavements, etc. In this case, different 'subscenarios' would be used to design the overall bridge; they would, most conveniently, be activated by their mother scenario. Notice that a bridge can also be viewed as an abstract object with an address, a state highway classification number, an architectural style, a maintenance cost per year, etc. Therefore, the level of abstractness of scenarios is dependent on the circumstances. Regarding design chiefly as a *geometric* activity has been the classical pitfall of the CAD systems and we want to take heed of that.

Scenarios, like frames, allow other looser principles such as the notion of 'similarity' between two scenarios. The easiest way to do this would be pattern matching; cf. Minsky (1975) for a detailed exposition of frame similarity and additional techniques to achieve it.

2.2   Modal and other nonstandard logics for design

Modal logic can be seen as the logic of *necessity* and *possibility* (Hughes and Cresswell, 1972). We shall show the basic notions that a system of modal logic is intended to express. We use the conventional notation for the modal operators, necessary and possible, and introduce new notation for the default and unknown operators.

Among true propositions we can distinguish between those that are merely true and that are bound to be true. Similarly, we can distinguish among false propositions between those that are bound to be false and those that are merely false. A proposition that is bound to be true is called a necessary proposition ($\mathbf{N}p$, it is necessary that p); one that is bound to be false is called an impossible proposition ($\mathbf{N} - p$, it is impossible that p). If a proposition is not impossible we call it a possible proposition ($\mathbf{P}p$, it is possible that p). We have now informally introduced the monadic proposition-forming operators $\mathbf{N}$ and $\mathbf{P}$. These operators are not truth-functional, i.e. the truth value of the proposition cannot be deduced even when the truth value of the argument is given. However, a strategy exists to determine the validity of a necessary or possible proposition. We do not give the exact definition of this validity checking but describe it informally.

A necessary proposition, $\mathbf{N}p$, is valid in a certain world iff p is valid in all worlds *accessible* to that world. A possible proposition, $\mathbf{P}p$, is valid in a certain world iff p is valid in one or more world(s) accessible to that world. Briefly, a world W_2 is accessible to a world W_1 if W_2 is conceivable by someone living in W_1. Consider the following example. We can conceive a world without telephones but if there had been no telephones, it would be the case that in such a world no-one would know about what a telephone was and so no-one would conceive of a world (e.g. ours) in which there are telephones (Hughes and Cresswell, 1972). More technically, suppose that we have a set of propositions. We can specify what the state of a world is by giving a list of which propositions are true and which are false according to this world. Let Ω be a dyadic reflexive relation over the worlds. Then Ω is called the accessibility relation, i.e. world w_i is accessible by w_j iff $w_i \, \Omega \, w_j$.

We use a different operator $\mathbf{D}$ to express *default* values. Thus, $\mathbf{D}p$ means that p is consistent with the theory. A proposition is consistent if its negation cannot be derived within the theory. A default proposition, $\mathbf{D}p$, is considered to be valid if $-p$ cannot be proved. With this mechanism, we have the possibility to deal with nonmonotonicity (McDermott, 1982). During the design process, some properties about the design object may not yet be known; so we can assume some default values. However, as soon as contradictory information is derived, we discard the default property and base things on the newly-obtained information. Notice that this is nothing but the well-known *truth-maintenance* problem (Doyle, 1979).

The modal operator $\mathbf{U}$ is used to denote uncertainty. A proposition is *unknown* if neither its truth nor its falsity can be derived. An unknown proposition, $\mathbf{U}p$, is considered to be valid if neither p nor $-p$ can be found. Note that we have now actually introduced a thrid truth value (i.e. unknown). The reason we avoid explicitly introducing a third truth value is that when we want to keep our logic as simple as possible. This further implies that we have the *open world* assumption (Mylopoulos and Levesque, 1984). Nevertheless, if we request p the knowledge base must return false if it finds $-p$ or cannot find p. Therefore, Up is required to know about the uncertainty of p.

2.3   Incomplete information and null values

Several ideas to be mentioned in this subsection owe their origin to recent research in databases. We follow especially Levesque (1984) and Reiter (1984) closely, for they too insist on using logic as a framework for databases.

Since our envisioned design system will be based on KE principles, the existence of a knowledge base (KB) is implicit as an integral part. Whatever supervisory mechanism (SPV) we have in the system, it would like to query the KB about a particular design application. In design, any KB would be incomplete since it is impossible to identify and store all the information necessary to answer a query. In this case, we should distinguish between what the KB knows and what the truths are in the design domain. A KB may know that a shaft is attached to a motor without knowing the motor's power rating; it may know that one of the cylinders of the motor is faulty without knowing which one. Thus, one cannot treat a design KB as a realistic replica of the application domain. Since design is an open-ended activity, it may turn out that design KBs will never stabilize and one should find ways to deal with this ever-changing character of them.

Assuming that logic is the underlying formalism, for each query κ there are four possibilities: (i) **true** when κ can be inferred from the KB, (ii) **false** when $-\kappa$ can be inferred from the KB, (iii) **unknown** when neither (i) nor (ii) holds, and (iv) **contradiction** when both (i) and (ii) hold. We call a KB *consistent* if it contains no contradictory information. In an *incomplete* KB, on the other hand, we may pose queries which have **unknown** as answer. Unknown information may be in several disguises. Consider the following example. We know that 'Door $D0023$ has a type $L0003$ or $L0014$ lock', but do not know which. A straightforward way to represent this fact is to have two interpretations of $D0023$: one with $L0003$, the other with $L0014$. Thus type of unknown is known in the database area as *disjunctive information*. Another common and more challenging unknown is the *null value*, meaning 'value at present unknown'. Now, if we accept the *closed world* assumption (i.e. the negation of any atomic formula can be inferred from the inability to infer the atomic formula, also known as *negation-by-failure* in Prolog) then solving the null-value problem is easy since it reduces to the disjunctive information problem with the disjuncts expressing all the possible values (collected from the KB). However, under the open world assumption the value will not necessarily be one of the same infinite set of known possible values. Consider the following. We know that 'Pipe $P0254$ feeds an oil tank' but do not know which. Moreover, this tank may or may not be one of the unknown tanks $T0001$ and $T0002$. In first-order theory, we would express this as

$$\exists X, \ oil\text{--}tank(X) \ \wedge \ fed\text{--}by(X, \ P0254)$$

then choose a name, ω, for this object and rewrite the preceding as

$$oil\text{--}tank(\omega) \ \wedge \ fed\text{--}by(\omega, \ P0254)$$

In fact, ω has long been known in the logic terminology as a *Skolem constant* and provides a way to eliminate the $\exists$ sign in proof theory; databases introduced the more suggestive name null values. It is important to observe that each time a new null value is introduced to the KB, it should be denoted by a new name (distinct from all other names). Thus, the switch below to $\hat{\omega}$ is compulsory to express 'Some tank (maybe the same one as *T0001* and *T0002*) is fed by pipe *P0789*':

$$oil\text{--}tank(\hat{\omega}) \ \wedge \ fed\text{--}by(\hat{\omega}, \ P0789)$$

In addition, the KB should be made aware of the existence of a null value in general. This means that the allowable entities (e.g. the universe made of *P0254*, *T0001*, *T0002* in the first example) must be expanded by introducing ω and the axioms should be revised as

$$\forall X, \ [oil\text{--}tank(X) \ \supset \ X \equiv T0001 \ \vee \ X \equiv T0002 \ \vee \ X \equiv \omega]$$

and

$$\forall X, \ Y, \ [fed\text{--}by(X, \ Y) \ \supset$$
$$(X \equiv T0001 \ \wedge \ Y \equiv P0245) \ \vee \ (X \equiv T0002 \ \wedge \ Y \equiv P0245) \ \vee \ (X \equiv \omega \ \wedge$$
$$Y \equiv P0245)]$$

2.4   Other nonstandard logics

Predicate calculus of higher order is useful to talk about inheritance. The following is provable in the second-order predicate logic: $\forall F, \ [F(x) \supset G(x)]$. (If an individual x has every property then x has any property G.) In third-order predicate logic, we can prove that $\forall F, \ [V(F) \supset V(G)]$. (Whatever is true of all functions of individuals is true of any function of individuals G.) While they are, theoretically speaking, well understood, the real challenge of higher-order logics lies in their implementation.

For temporal logic, we can use the following notation. Let $t \ \alpha \ p$ denote that p holds *after* time t and $t \ \beta \ p$ denote that p holds *before* time t; $[t_1, \ t_2]$ denotes a time interval. Several useful equalities can be written:

$$t \alpha -p = -(t \alpha p)$$
$$t \alpha (p \wedge q) = t \alpha p) \wedge (t \alpha q)$$
$$[t_1, t_2] \alpha p = (t_1 \beta p) \wedge (t_2 \beta_p) \wedge (t_1 < t_2)$$

Using temporal logic, we can describe inference control for our system in a more explicit way. For instance, in Prolog the order of rules matters (Bobrow, 1985). In general, this knowledge is embedded in the interpreter of this language. By disclosing this control we may introduce suppler control. As an example, 'detailing' knowledge for a design object may be a set of rules of the sort

$$(t_1 \alpha q_1) \wedge (t_2 \alpha q_1) \wedge (t_1 < t_2) \supset t_2 \alpha q_3$$
$$(t_1 \alpha q_1) \wedge (t_2 \alpha q_2) \wedge (t_2 < t_1) \supset t_2 \alpha q_4$$

where the q_i are understood in the sense of section 2.1.

Intuitionistic logic can also be incorporated into temporal logic. let t_p be the time when proposition p is proved. By definition, we have $t_p \alpha p = $ **true**. Now using the logical symbol **unknown** we can formalize intuitionism in terms of temporality:

$$t_p \beta (p \vee -p) = \textbf{unknown}, t_p \alpha (p \vee -p) = \textbf{true}$$

We note that incorporating the complete functionalities of these assorted logics may very well result in high (even intractable) computational complexity. To avoid this, we must include only those functionalities that are relevant to our design requirements. For example, in the case of temporality we may be satisfied with only α and β although there is surely more to temporal logic than these simple operators.

Once we extend the first-order predicate logic with these operators, we have a powerful notation to describe design knowledge in a flexible manner. Since a design object is constantly updated during the design process, we need to describe it in a dynamic way. The constructs we have envisioned above work with a multiword mechanism realized in modal logic. This mechanism helps the designer describe a design object seen from several viewpoints and express default and uncertain information about a design object.

3. THE METHOD OF EXTENSIONS/INTENSIONS

3.1 Philosophical origins

We begin with a philosophical discussion about knowledge representation and then move to more concrete issues. We start with a definition of *L-truth*, a notion also known as logical truth, necessary truth (Leibniz), and analytic truth (Kant). The subject matter is historical and treated in great detail in Carnap (1947). Call a sentence, σ, L-true in a system, Σ, iff σ is true in Σ in such a way that its truth can be established on the basis of the rules of the system Σ alone, without reference to (extra-linguistic) facts. This is, in a sense, what Leibniz meant when he stated 'A necessary truth must hold in all possible worlds.'

It is customary to regard two *classes*, say those corresponding to the predicates p and q, identical if they have the same elements (e.g. p and q are equivalent). By the *intension* of the predicate p we mean the property p; by its *extension* we mean the corresponding class. The term *property* is understood in an objective (physical) sense, not in a subjective, mental sense. Thus 'red' table should mean that the colour of the table (as understood, in the final analysis, as a physical property) is red, not that the person who is looking at it perceives it (for some e.g. psychological reason) as red. Thus, one may state that the table has the character Red whereas the observer has the character Red-Seeing. A good account of intensions and extensions is given in the following passage:

> 'Class may be defined either extensionally or intensionally. That is to say, we may define the kind of object which is a class, or the kind of concept which denotes a class: this is the precise meaning of the opposition of extension and intension in this connection. But although the general notion can be defined in this two-fold manner, particular classes, except when they happen to be finite, can only be defined intensionally, i.e. as the objects denoted by such and such concepts. I believe this distinction to be purely psychological: logically, the extensional definition appears to be equally applicable to infinite classes, but practically, if we were to attempt it, Death would cut short our laudable endeavour before it had attained its goal. Logically, therefore, extension and intension seem to be on a par' (Bertrand Russell).

For example, let S denote that something is a shaft and let L denote that something is two miles long. The conjunction $S \wedge L$ would mean that something is a shaft and two miles long — denoting an empty yet not meaningless class. On the other hand, $S \wedge - S$ would mean shaft and at the same time not shaft — an L-empty statement. No factual knowledge is required for recognizing the fact that the last conjunction cannot be exemplified.

The method of intensions/extensions has its roots in the work of Frege who studied it in a less rigorous way and called it the method of *name-relation*. This consists of regarding expressions as names of (concrete or abstract) entities in accordance with the following principles:

- Every name has exactly one entity named by it, i.e. its *nominatum.*
- Any sentence speaks about the nominata of the names occurring in it.
- If a name occurring in a true sentence is replaced by another name with the same nominatum, the sentence remains true.

If the last principle is applied without restriction, contradictions may arise. Frege's solution was to draw a distinction between the nominatum and the 'sense' of an expression. A classical example is the two expressions 'the morning star' and 'the evening star.' Although these expressions have the same nominatum they certainly do not have the same sense. It will be seen that nominatum resembles extension and sense resembles intension. (In fact, John Stuart Mill used the more descriptive terms denotation and connotation, respectively, for the above concepts.)

3.2 Describing design entities

We find the main use of intensions/extensions in describing design objects. Suppose that we are trying to describe a pressure regulator. Normally, we would have a 'method' which knows about a certain type of pressure regulator, possibly parametrized so that one can create (i.e. design) instances of it by changing the parameters. Thus, e.g.

$$pres\text{–}reg(max\text{–}pressure, max\text{–}deviation, input\text{–}area, output\text{–}area,$$
$$valve\text{–}type, \ldots)$$

would be the way this method could be invoked. The suggestion is to visualize this as an intensional description. The method *pres-reg* comprises all the information one would require to deal with this kind of regulator. In that sense, it *embodies* the concept of a regulator. This makes it efficient in terms of design time since all the knowledge is there and one simply has to make the right invocation of this method. On the other hand this intensional description is inflexible since if one now wants to add a new 'parameter', e.g. *max-fluid-viscosity*, one would face the problem of studying and changing the whole method.

An extensional description of the same regulator is a collection of facts of the sort:

$$pres\text{–}reg(PR)$$
$$input\text{–}area(PR, area_{in})$$
$$output\text{–}area(PR, area_{out})$$
$$max\text{–}deviation(PR, max\text{–}dev)$$
$$max\text{–}pressure(PR, max\text{–}pres)$$
$$valve\text{–}type(PR, v\text{–}type)$$
$$\ldots$$

and some procedural knowledge to structure these. Now adding the new fact would be just the addition of the new piece of information *max-fluid-viscosity(PR, max-vis)*. Obviously, the procedural parts should also change but this change is thought to be smaller and much more 'local'. It is not difficult to see, on the other hand, that this new method of describing the regulator suffers from inefficiency since there are several facts that should be combined in some way, i.e. the available information is in bits and pieces and should be put together.

For design, the advantage of extensional descriptions should be clear. In design, we need an integrated set of models each of which represents a different facet of the design object and possibly changes during the design process. From this viewpoint, intensional descriptions are very rigid and data exchange between two different, say, solid modelling systems based on these description methods may suffer from loss of information or distortion of meaning.

4.   NAIVE PHYSICS: A THEORY OF DESIGN OBJECTS?

We shall keep this section short since we are in the process of preparing a longer reply to the question posed in the section title.

4.1   Expressing naive physics knowledge

Since its inception by Patrick Hayes a decade ago (Hayes, 1985), naive physics (NP) has established itself as an exciting branch of AI. The aim of NP is to represent and simulate the knowledge and thought processes humans have about the physical world. A good example is attributed to Marvin Minsky: 'You can pull with a string but not push with it.' While we possess such trivial knowledge it is exceedingly difficult to have computers appreciate and use it. Giving such commonsense physical knowledge to computers is essentially the aim of NP.

An integral part of NP is qualitative reasoning (QR) about the physical processes. This can best be explained with an example. Consider a sealed container full of water. If it is subjected to heat, it will eventually explode. The process that gives rise to this is the transformation of water into steam which applies huge forces. In this style of reasoning we are not really interested in the nuts and bolts of what is going on, i.e. we are hardly interested the 'exact' physical relationships, equations, constants, etc., ultimately leading to this explosion. Qualitative physics (we prefer NP to this term) is a special kind of physics where we use QR instead of dealing with exact mathematical relationships. The main reason for this is that exact mathematical analysis is not what human beings are thought to perform in ordinary circumstances. A more technical reason is that exact analysis is sometimes exceedingly difficult and even impossible (e.g. nonlinear differential equations).

Why are NP notions such as solids, liquids, force, time, etc., useful in design? The answer is that design objects will, when manufactured, exist in the physical world where the above notions will be in effect. Why do we need QR? There may be several answers but one good reason is that we want to determine the impact of unanticipated changes on an object in its destined environment. The common example here is an event such as the Three-Mile Island accident where it is now believed that a simple, clear way of reasoning qualitatively about the physical processes and changes leading to a catastrophe would possibly prevent a similar accident.

A long time ago Hayes (1985) proposed that one should use logic in describing NP knowledge. We plan to take this route. For example, we have good examples which demonstrate the suitability of modal logic in encoding situational calculus. (Imagine e.g. modelling the possible outcomes of envisionment (de Kleer and Brown, 1984) with the help of the possible worlds of modal logic.) As an additional tool, we want to use the 'chunking' of knowledge — as done, for example, by de Kleer (1975) in his restricted access local consequent methods (RALCMs) — to collect together and use physical formulas intelligently. (Note that this can be done by using a class for each chunk). For QR, the need for a symbolic algebra based on confluences is immediate (de Kleer and Brown, 1984).

While in QR we have a reasonably complete mathematical model of a situation, this itself is never sufficient for many tasks. QR is expected to interpret the numerical values of several problem variables. Assume that p is a quantity directly proportional to the quotient r/t. If r increases while t stays constant or decreases, a QR system can draw the useful conclusion that p increases. However, consider the case of both r and t increasing, albeit with unknown rates. In this case, a QR system is helpless unless it can read the values from some measuring device and do numerical computation. This need to switch back and forth between traditional computing and qualitative analysis has paved the way to coupled systems.

4.2   Coupled systems for expert computation

One of the main uses of computers since their invention (and in fact, one of the reasons for their invention) has been 'numerical' computation. It is difficult to define what is exactly *numerical* (as opposed to symbolic) but it may suffice to point out that most of the numerical-analysis libraries such as IMSDL^{TM} are full of numerical code — code that computes integrals, multiplies or inverts matrices, solves differential equations, etc. One unifying property of these libraries is that they work on numbers and they produce numbers. *Symbolic* computation systems such as MACSYMA^{TM}, on the other hand, work on symbols and produce symbols.

If 'the aim of computing is insight, not numbers', as Richard Hamming has been quoted to advise, then numerical code provides little help to give insights to what is going on, especially in huge computational tasks. More often than not, one gets, after hours of computation, a long list of numbers which hardly say anything explicitly (thus necessitating a post-computational period when the results are 'analysed') or, quite disturbingly, messages like 'underflow while computing M^{-1}'.

Traditionally, numerical computing has been used in data processing, simulations, statistics, etc., whereas symbolic computing was employed in data interpretation, cognitive modelling, search and heuristics, and nondeterministic problem-solving. It should be added that by using the term symbolic computing we do not confine ourselves to symbolic algebra systems. Many familiar expert systems (e.g. Mycin, Prospector, Dendral) have symbolic computation facilities while they would not be regarded as computer algebra systems. An informal definition would then equate numerical computing with 'number crunching' intensive processes while symbolic computing is understood as logic, heuristic, and reason-intensive.

A *coupled* system 'must have some knowledge of the numerical processes embedded within them and reason about the application or results of those numerical processes' (Kitzmiller and Kowalik, 1986). It is natural to assume that in a coupled system a symbolic supervisor is at the top level, scheduling the numerical processes. Such a supervisor would have knowledge about the process's aim, input/output behavior, run-time limitations (e.g. the smallest and largest numbers it can deal with; truncation characteristics), and so on.

We close this subsection with a general remark about the necessity of coupled systems. Consider the design of a complex artifact such as a nuclear reactor or a space shuttle. On the symbolic side there is a need for database management, truth maintenance, computing with constraint equations, answering 'what-if' questions (possibly for testing and fault simulation), etc. On the numerical side, there is a need to have expert knowledge about computational mechanics, fluid dynamics, earthquake engineering, materials science, Monte-Carlo techniques, etc. Human designers solve problems of this scale with a careful mix of symbolic and numerical techniques. Without a strong coupling of symbolic and numerical code, the automation of these complex tasks cannot be expected.

5.   COMBINING OBJECT-ORIENTED AND LOGIC PROGRAMMING

5.1   Why are we doing this?

Logic languages such as Prolog provide the means to deal with a KB of facts; they especially come up with a uniform computational mechanism such as unification to execute logic formulas. Object-oriented languages such as Smalltalk (Goldberg, 1983) use encapsulation to structure data and employ message-passing as the underlying computational principle (Stefik and Bobrow, 1986).

An obvious shortcoming of existing logic languages is the overhead of an extensive database which is physically homogeneous. This has the result that, without some metalevel control, query evaluation may become hopelessly inefficient when the database is bulky. Another weakness is the lack of abstract data types. For existing object-oriented languages a major symptom of unsuitability for CAD has been the fixed (run-time) structure of the inheritance lattice. It is normally impossible to declare new objects which reside somewhere between the already-existing parents and children. This normally takes us to issues such as inheritance vs. delegation which we want to avoid at present, despite their importance.

We hope that our draft proposal of a language to overcome these difficulties is pointing more or less in the right direction to combine the paradigms of logic and object-orientation. We have enumerated the requirements (originating from our desire to use it to code design knowledge) for this language in Veth (1987a) and, for brevity, shall not repeat them here. For another account of how to combine programming paradigms (the story of Loops) we refer the reader to Stefik *et al*. (1986).

5.2   IDDL, a design base language

In IDDL, constants and variables denote entities. They are both called *objects*. A predicate denotes a relationship among entities and attributes which are expressed by functions. A function represents an attribute of an entity. Note that it is possible to define a function even on a set of predicates. Function-definition can be done by procedures.

Logical implication and equivalence are literally so and work as a *watchdog* in the KB. Suppose that there is a clause $p(XC) \rightarrow q(X)$ denoting the transformation rule that as soon as, e.g. $p(a)$ is found, $q(a)$ must be added to the KB. (Logical equivalence performs this bidirectionally.) Note that, since we employ intuitionistic logic, we do not assume $- p(a)$ even when $- q(a)$ is asserted. In the same way, deleting $p(a)$ does not imply deleting $q(a)$ or any other fact derived from $p(a)$.

There are two temporal connectives: *before* and *after*. There will be no two facts asserted at the same time. Therefore, these connectives form a fact set with complete ordering. Every object, well-formed formula, etc., has a set of information about its origin, destination, and time stamp. These are used by the SPV for controlling the inference.

Modal operators based on the system T (Hughes and Cresswell, 1972) are available, i.e. $\#N$ (necessity) and $\#P$ (possibility). Since these two are based on the system T, they precede only predicates. There is an 'unknown' operator, %, which can precede only atomic predicates. The $\#D$ default operator is another modal operator and can precede only atomic predicates. The necessity and possibility operators deal with different worlds whereas the default operator deals with nonmonotonicity or truth-maintenance within one world.

Two quantifiers are available: $\#A$ for the universal quantifier $\forall$ and $\#E$ for the existential quantifier $\exists$. A clause is defined by a list of predicates combined by connectives. Clauses and rules can be quantified.

IDDL is based on intuitionistic logic which implies further the open world assumption. Thus, IDDL uses, deep in its heart, three-valued logic including the unknown truth value rather than the conventional two-valued logic. Intuitionism means that, to check a fact, unless one has positive evidence, one is not able to say yes. The open world assumption is considered in terms of the **unknown** modal operator on the level of IDDL programs. Three-valued logic including **unknown** besides **true** and **false** is employed only internally. This means that the KB and the SPV distinguish **false** and **unknown** but logically these two values are treated the same. The unknown truth value is explicitly handled by the unknown modal operator. Thus, $\%p(a)$ returns **true** when there is no $p(a)$ and $- p(a)$.

IDDL has the concept of a *world*. It is defined as a partition of the KB such that worlds are independent from each other but can be linked so that changes in one world can propagate to others. There must always be at least one currently-active world in the KB. Worlds are subject to manipulation. A world consists of (i) objects, (ii) facts, and (iii) available functions. A world is created or declared with these elements. There are *global* worlds and *local* worlds. Local worlds are defined as those belonging to scenarios. Global worlds persist in the KB forever until explicitly removed, while local worlds automatically disappear after the execution of scenarios.

Two types of action are possible: pure *enquiries* and *assertions*. Suppose that we want to ask the KB $p(X)$. If there is $p(a)$ and $p(b)$ then X is instantiated to the set $\{a, b\}$ and **true** is returned. If there are no such facts in the KB, X remains unstantiated and **false** is returned. Consider now the inquiry $- p(a, b)$. If $p(a. b)$ is found, **true** is returned; however, if $p(a, b)$ is found, **false** is returned. If neither $- p(a, b)$ nor $p(a, b)$ is found, **unknown** is returned.

$\#N$ and $\#P$ are used to deal with different (currently-active) worlds. $- Np(a)$ returns **true** when all the currently-active worlds have $p(a)$; if there are some worlds where $- p(a)$ is found, **false** is returned. If some or all of the active worlds do not have $p(a)$, **unknown** is returned. $\#Pp(a)$ returns **true** when there is at least one active world which has $p(a)$; **false** is returned when all the active worlds have $- p(a)$. If there is neither $p(a)$ nor $- p(a)$ in the active worlds then **unknown** is returned.

A fact such as $\#Dp(a)$ matches $\#Dp(a)$ and returns **true**. Otherwise, it returns **false** (because the problem is whether $p(a)$ is qualified by $\#D$ or not). Assertions, on the other hand, are associated with modifying the KB. Again consider asking $p(X)$. If there exist $p(a)$ and $p(b)$, X is instantiated to the set $\{a, b\}$ and **true** is returned. In this case the assertion *succeeded*. If there is no such fact in the current worlds, an object which is referenced by X is created and this fact is added to the current worlds. Finally, **true** is returned as the logical value of this assertion to indicate that it succeeded. By assertion one may create new objects. The assertion $p(a)$ *fails*, when there is already $- p(a)$ in the current worlds. We note that & (logical and) and | (logical or) operators are different in terms of assertion. For example, consider the assertions of $p(a) \& q(a)$ and $p(a) | q(a)$. The and operator puts both $p(a)$ and $q(a)$ in the currently-active worlds. If either of them fails, the whole assertion fails. On the other hand, the or operator creates a copy of the currently active world and puts $p(a)$ and $q(a)$ separately into the original world and the copied world. Having an or operator on the right-hand side (RHS) of a rule, one implicitly creates a new world. If both of these assertions fail, the whole assertion fails.

There is a built-in predicate *assert* which explicitly does an assertion. This predicate is, by definition, a higher-order predicate. Enquiries are specified by the built-in predicate *inquire*. The opposite of *assert* is *remove* which retracts a fact from the KB. In case there is an equivalence definition in the KB, by asserting a fact an equivalent fact might be added to the KB automatically. However, this will not happen when a fact is removed.

By asserting $\#Np(a)$, all currently-active worlds will have $p(a)$ and the assertion will succeed. If there are some worlds where $- p(a)$ is found, the assertion fails. By asserting $\#Pp(a)$, all the active worlds will have either $p(a)$ or $\#Dp(a)$. Worlds which already have $- p(a)$ are not touched. However, if all the active worlds already have $- p(a)$, the assertion fails. Whern a fact qualified by the default modal operator $\#Dp(a)$ is asserted, $p(a)$ is put into the current worlds and labelled as *default*. Facts which are derived from those default facts will be labelled as *derived facts* (from $p(a)$). Sometime in the future, if $p(a)$ is asserted then these labels will be removed. If $- p(a)$ is asserted in the future, all the assumed facts and derived facts will be removed from the current worlds and $- p(a)$ is asserted instead.

A rule has the well-known *if-then* syntax. Note that there is no logical implication in a rule; this is completel;y different from the $\rightarrow$ operator. Rules will be purely procedurally interpreted by the SPV. A rule is interpreted as 'if *clause-1* is true, then *clause-2* must hold'. Thus, unless specified, the following is expected by default. If *clause-1* is found, then *clause-2* is asserted. For the left-hand side (LHS) parts of rules, normally clauses are regarded as inquiries. For the RHS parts, assertions are assumed unless explicitly specified (such as just an enquiry). If it is impossible to assert the entire clause, the assertion fails. If, for one reason or another, the assertion on the RHS fails, it is taken that the rule has failed.

An *instantiation list* is used to keep track of 'once-matched facts' so that they will not fire again. Quantifiers are used to talk about objects instantiated to variables. Consider an enquiry $p(X) \rightarrow q(X)$ and facts $p(a)$, $p(b)$, $p(c)$, $q(a)$, and $q(b)$ in the KB. $\#A[X]p[X] \rightarrow q(X)$ returns **unknown** since there is no $p(c)$. On the other hand, $\#E[X]p(X) \rightarrow q(X)$ returns **true** and its instantiation list in this case is $\{a, b\}$. In IDDL quantifiers can also quantify rules.

If on the LHS there are facts labelled *default* or *derived-from*, the facts on the RHS will be asserted with the label *derived-from* the fact in the LHS. By doing so, one keeps track of assumed facts (i.e. truth maintenance).

A scenario is defined as a set of rules. A scenario (or a scenario base) is a set of scenarios. A scenario has the following elements:

- scenario name (*List-of-Worlds*)
- flow declaration reference (to resolve the destination references)
- world declaration reference, which further consists of:
  - object declaration reference
  - function declaration reference
- object declaration reference
- function declaration reference
- rules

A scenario is active when the control is passed to it by the SPV or another scenario. The argument *List–of–Worlds* defines worlds passed by the caller. A scenario can have those *imported* worlds as well as local worlds declared in the world declaration references. There is a world called *default-world* which can be used without declaration and is local only to that scenario. Object and function declarations on the same level as the world declaration belong to this local world, *default-world*. The object declaration in a world defines local objects which can be used only in that world. Global objects are declared as local objects of a global world. From scenarios there must be a reference to those global objects. Local objects will never be seen from upper level scenarios. The idea of object declaration almost corresponds to the idea of 'typing' in conventional languages.

Worlds cannot be accessed from scenarios which have no declarations referring to them. In case a scenario has more than two worlds, which world is to be considered is specified by the *enter* built-in predicate. (The opposite is the *exit* predicate.) Note that one cannot switch worlds that are created by an | operator. These copied worlds are equally treated as the original worlds. By declaring objects in the object declaration part, the current world contains only those declared objects. Two or more worlds can share objects by *referring* or by *importing/exporting*. This takes place in such a way that a declared object and its relevant clauses and functions associated with objects are automatically collected and put into the current world.

A world can be treated by the *enclose(World, List-of-Objects)* built-in predicate. This predicate creates a new world called *World* with *List-of-Objects*. This is an enclosure mechanism. After the enclosure, the enclosed world will be treated as an object. The type of *World* is defined by its object declaration. Whether *World* is global or local is dependent on that. After enclosure, the contents of the world can be accessed only by functions. The enclosure mechanism can be, therefore, perceived as 'intensionalizing extensions', and functions are used to 'find the anatomy' of an enclosed world. Similarly, it is not far-fetched to regard functions as equivalent to messages.

A scenario will be executed in the following way. Examining the rules from the top, the first rule whose LHS is satisfied is selected. Then the RHS of this rule is asserted. If the assertion is successful, search for the next matching rule starts with the rule following the previously-executed rule. If the assertion fails, once again search starts and another rule will be selected. If the execution terminates successfully, all the results will be preserved. In case of failure, all the results will be removed. If the search for the next applicable rule comes back to the most recently executed rule because the search 'wraps around', it is judged that there are no applicable rules and the execution of the entire scenario stops (i.e. *no-more-rule* situation). The execution of a scenario can also be stopped by the execution of either *success* or *fail* built-in predicates. When a scenario terminates successfully, worlds related to that scenario are preserved. When a scenario terminates unsuccessfully, related worlds are removed from the KB. When a rule is selected, an instantiation list is created. This list is preserved until the end of the execution of the entire scenario so that the same rule will not be applied to the identical objects in the same situation.

One can 'open' an object and regard it as a world (called by the name of the object). This is done by the *open* built-in predicate. To leave that world, one can use the *close* built-in predicate. The former assumes the *enter* predicate, and the latter assumes *exit* as a prerequisite. A *select* predicate changes the active scenario to a new one and restricts the active objects used in that scenario to *List-of-Objects*. In case this list is empty, the active objects are not restricted. On the other hand, a *use* predicate adds the new scenario name ot the active scenario and restricts the active objects used to *List-of-Objects*. This predicate, therefore, enlarges the set of available rules. The last two predicates can be true when the subscenario is finished by the execution of a *success* built-in predicate or by the no-more-rule situation. They can be false when the subscenario is explicitly terminated by the execution of a *fail*. This means 'selection' switches active scenarios while 'using' shows details of the currently-manipulated objects via more dedicated rules. These two predicates are important to realize the so-called 'multiworld mechanism' of section 2.1. Finally, in order to restrict active objects without changing scenarios, one can use the predicates *consider-(List-of-Objects)* and *unconsider(List-of-Objects)*.

6. SUMMARIZING REMARKS AND FUTURE DIRECTIONS

The aim of our work is to develop an integrated, interactive, and intelligent computer-aided design system. IIICAD will be a generic system which may be used in any design domain and will incorporate three types of design knowledge. First, the system has general knowledge about the design processes based on a set-theoretic design theory. Second, it has domain-dependent knowledge belonging to a specific area (e.g. VLSI) where it is actually used. Third, the system maintains knowledge about previously designed entities. This kind of history mechanism enables the system to reuse its knowledge in the forthcoming design activities. It is useful to imagine this as a variant of software re-use.

The project is divided into several areas of interest in which different AI techniques are used:

- Formalization of general design theory; modal and other nonstandard logics as a knowledge representation language.
- Commonsense reasoning about the physical world (naive physics) and coupled systems.
- Integration of object-oriented and logic programming paradigms.

As a result, a formal definition of a kernel language for design will be generated. This language for integrated data description (called IDDL) will be used to implement the IIICAD system. IDDL, equipped with nonstandard logics, enables the IIICAD system to describe design knowledge and to control the design process in a highly expressive and robust manner. In section 5.2, we gave a taste of IDDL; cf. Veth (1987c) for full draft specifications. Formalization of the design theory will take place by means of frame-like structures called scenarios. We use general design theory (Tomigama and Yoshikawa, 1987) as a basis for formalizing design processes and knowledge.

The NP and QR knowledge which will be used during the design process performs commonsense reasoning about the physical world. Depending on the phase of the design process, the declaration of the physical qualities of a design object takes place in logic and by means of references to physical laws. Interfacing between the IIICAD system and already-existing qualitative systems (such as ENVISION (de Kleer and Brown, 1984) and QSIM (Kuipers, 1986) should also be studied, in our future work.

Declaration of knowledge about a design object may be done by logically manipulating the object's attributes. At the same time, the knowledge itself refers to the specific behaviour of the object. These two characteristics lead to a need to integrate object-oriented and logical programming styles into one language. One of the major areas of interest within IIICAD therefore, is to find out how this integration is to be achieved (i.e. multi-paradigm languages) and what additional properties our draft proposal, IDDL, should have.

Finally, a few words about the project schedule. The project was planned to span three years, with the first year being devoted to research on the theories of knowledge, design processes, and design objects. The first concrete outcome of this research was IDDL (Vath, 1987c). The second year was devoted to developing a first version of the IIICAD using a rapid prototyping approach. We are using the Smalltalk-80^{TM} (Goldberg, 1983) programming environment to implement IDDL (and IIICAD) and regard Smalltalk's excellent user interface and debugging tools as major aids for software development on this scale. The system design consists of various components such as a KB, an intelligent user interface, a supervisor to control the design processes and information flow, a common sense reasoner, etc.

We seek further discussion of IDDL and would welcome feedback.

'What has happened to the design "guru"? Didn't every design and development engineering department once have one? At one of my first jobs the department manager and his assistant sat in their glassed-in offices in one corner of our lab. The rest of us each had our 8-foot section of bench. Except for our guru. He sat outside the bosses' offices at a desk of his very own. And while we toiled at 'scopes and breadboards, he didn't do anything. Nothing, that is, except answer questions the rest of us could not.' (Christiansen, 1987).

ACKNOWLEDGEMENTS

The authors are members of Group *Bart Veth* which additionally includes Peter Bernus (CWI) and Tetsuo Tomiyama (University of Tokyo). Acknowledgements are made to NFI for its support of IIICAD and to Tomiyama, Monique Megens (CWI), and Eric Weijers (CWI) for their invaluable contributions to the project.

IMSL is a trademark of IMSL, Inc. MACSYMA is a trademark of Symbolics, Inc. Smalltalk-80 is a trademark of Xerox Corp. Mention of commercial products in this chapter does not imply endorsement.

REFERENCES

Bobrow, D. (1985) If Prolog is the answer, what is the question? or What it takes to support AI programming paradigms. *IEEE Trans. Software Engineering* **11**(11), 1401–1408.

Bobrow, D., Mittal, S., and Stefik, M. (1986) Expert systems: perils and promise. *Communications of the ACM* **29**(9), 880–894.

Brown, D. C. and Chandrasekaran, B. (1986) Knowledge and control for a mechanical design expert system. *IEEE Computer* **19**(7), 92–100.

Carnap, R. (1947) *Meaning and necessity: A Study in Semantics and Modal Logic*, The Univ. of Chicago Press, Chicago, Ill.

Christiansen, D. (1987) On good designers. *IEEE Spectrum (Special report: On good design)* **24**(5), 25.

Doyle, J. (1979) A truth maintenance system. *Artificial Intelligence* **12**, 231–272.

Dyer, M. G., Flowers, M., and Hodges, J. (1986) EDISON: an engineering design invention system operating naively. *Artificial Intelligence in Engineering* **1**(1), 36–44.

Gero, J. S. (ed.) (1985) *Knowledge Engineering in Computer-Aided Design*, North-Holland, Amsterdam.

Gero, J. S. (ed.) (1987) *Expert Systems for Computer Aided Design*, North-Holland, Amsterdam.

Goldberg, A. (1983) *Smalltalk-80: the Interactive Programming Environment*, Addison-Wesley, Reading, Mass.

Hayes, P. (1985) The second naive physics manifesto. pp. 1–36 in *Formal Theories of the Commonsense World,* ed. J. Hobbs and R. Moore, Ablex, Norwood, New Jersey.

Hughes, G. E. and Cresswell, M. J. (1972) *An Introduction to Modal Logic*, Methuen, London.

Kitzmiller, C. T. and Kowalik, J. S. (1986) Symbolic and numerical computing in knowledge based systems. pp. 3–17 in *Coupling Symbolic and Numerical Computing in Expert Systems*, ed. J. S. Kowalik, Elsevier, Amsterdam.

de Kleer, J. (1975) Qualitative and quantitative knowledge in classical mechanics. *AI-TR-352*, Artificial Intelligence Lab., MIT, Cambridge, Mass.

de Kleer, J. and Brown, J. S. (1984) A qualitative physics based on confluences. *Artificial Intelligence* **24**, 7–83.

Kuipers, B. (1986) Qualitative simulation. *Artificial Intelligence* **29**, 289–338.

Lansdown, J. (1988) Graphics, design, and artificial intelligence. in *Theoretical Foundations of Computer Graphics and CAD*, ed. R. A. Earnshaw, NATO ASI Series, Springer-Verlag, Heidelberg.

Levesque, H. J. (1984) The logic of incomplete knowledge bases. pp. 165–189 in *On Conceptual Modelling (Perspectives from Artificial Intelligence, Databases, and Programming Languages)*, ed. M. L. Brodie, J. Mylopoulos and J. W. Schmidt, Springer-Verlag, New York.

McDermott, D. (1975) Nonmonotonic logic II: Nonmonotonic modal theories. *Journal of ACM* **29**(1), 33–57.

Minsky, M. (1975) A framework for representing knowledge. pp. 211–277 in *The Psychology of Computer Vision,* ed. P. Winston, McGraw-Hill, New York.

Mittal, S., Dym, C. L., and Morjaria, M. (1986) PRIDE: An expert system for the design of paper handling systems. *IEEE Computer* **19**(7), 102–114.

Moore, R. C. (1985) The role of logic in knowledge representation and commonsense reasoning. pp. 336–341 in *Readings in Knowledge Representation*, ed. R. J. Brachman and H. J. Levesque, Morgan Kaufmann, Los Altos, Calif.

Mylopoulos, J. and Levesque, H. J. (1984) An overview of knowledge representations. pp. 3–17 in *On Conceptual Modelling (Perspectives from Artificial Intelligence, Databases, and Programming Languages)*, ed. M. L. Brodie, J. Mylopoulos and J. W. Schmidt, Springer-Verlag, New York.

Reiter, R. (1984) Towards a logical reconstruction of relational database theory. pp. 191–233 in *On Conceptual Modelling (Perspectives from Artificial Intelligence, Databases, and Programming Languages)*, ed. M. L. Brodie, J. Mylopoulos and J. W. Schmidt, Springer-Verlag, New York.

Skylar, J. (1987) A cut above: a manufacturer of lawnmower engines pushes computer-aided design software to new limits. *Logic (a publication of Control Data)*, pp. 3–7.

Stefik, M. and Bobrow, D. (1986) Object oriented programming: themes and variations. *AI Magazine* **6**(4), pp. 40–62.

Stefik, M., Bobrow, D., and Kahn, K. (1986) Integrating access oriented programming with a multiparadigm environment. *IEEE Software* **3**(1), 10–18.

ten Hagen, P. and Tomiyama, T. (eds.) (1987) *Intelligent CAD Systems 1: Theoretical and Methodological Aspects*, Springer-Verlag, Heidelberg.

Tomiyama and ten Hagen, P. (1987a) Representing knowledge in two distinct descriptions: extensional vs. intensional. *CWI Report CS-R8728*, Centre for Mathematics and Computer Science, Amsterdam.

Tomiyama, T. and ten Hagen, P. (1987b) The concept of intelligent integrated interactive CAD systems. *CWI Report CS-R8717*, Centre for Mathematics and Computer Science, Amsterdam.

Tomiyama, T. and ten Hagen, P. (1987c) Organization of design knowledge in an intelligent CAD environment. in *Expert Systems for Computer-Aided Design*, ed. J. Gero, North-Holland, Amsterdam.

Tomiyama, T. and Yoshikawa, H. (1987) Extended general design theory. pp. 95–130 in *Design Theory for CAD*, ed. H. Yoshikawa and E. A. Warman, North-Holland, Amsterdam.

Veth, B. (1987a) An integrated data description language for coding design knowledge. in *Intelligent CAD Systems 1: Theoretical and Methodological Aspects*, ed. P. ten Hagen and T. Tomiyama, Springer-Verlag, Heidelberg.

Veth, B. (1987b) Design as a formal, knowledge engineered activity. *CWI Report*, Centre for Mathematics and Computer Science, Amsterdam.

Veth, B. (1987c) IDDL, an integrated data description language. *CWI Report*, Centre for Mathematics and Computer Science, Amsterdam.

Yoshikawa, H. and Warman, E. A. (eds) (1987) *Design Theory for CAD*, North-Holland, Amsterdam.

Part IV
Expert systems applications

9

Design and operation of an expert system prototype for fault analysis in electrical nets

M. Emaldi, J. A. Fernandez Tellechea, I. Laresgoiti, J. Pérez
LABEIN, Electronics Dept., Cuesta de Olabeaga 16, 48013
Bilbao, Spain
J. Amantegui and **J. Echávarri**
IBERDUERO S.A., Gardoqui 8, 48008 Bilbao, Spain

SUMMARY

There are many references in the literature to research prototypes of expert systems (ESs) for industrial applications, but not so many about actual systems in operation. In this chapter we describe their differences from dialogue-oriented ESs (MYCIN-like), as well as the architecture and first operational results obtained with LAIDA, a first prototype of an ES for on-line fault analysis in electrical high-voltage power networks. The system is actually installed at the Dispatch Centre, linked to the existing SCADA equipment.

1. INTRODUCTION

The LAIDA project is being developed by LABEIN (a research and development laboratory sponsored by the Basque Government) and IBER-DUERO S.A. (an electric utility in Spain). It involves the development of an expert system (ES) which analyses alarm messages generated by disturbances in IBERDUERO's electrical power network.

Traditionally, ESs have an interactive nature (Shortliffe, 1976; Smith and Baker, 1983), since it was the user who provided all the information required for the reasoning process, therefore filtering the information in two ways;

— The system receives the user's own judgement and interpretation of the situation under inspection.
— The amount of information transferred is limited by his/her typing ability.

Furthermore, neither dynamic system evolution nor time considerations of the situation are taken into account.

This approach is not feasible for industrial applications such as maintenance, process control or supervision, since the amount of data is both too
large and time-related; the system does a time-dependent and often time-
critical analysis. This concept is not just an extension of traditional methodologies, but requires a substantial amount of research on new methodologies
and tools.

LAIDA follows this second approach, and is what we call a second-
generation ES since it was designed with the following operating principles
in mind:

— It operates on-line.
— It collects evolving and time-dependent data in real time, instead of
   waiting for the operator to provide it.
— It must react in pseudo-real-time, so that its advice comes out in time for
   the operator to use it in order to recover the network's full operation
   efficiently.

A number of projects are being developed today which are related to ours,
either because they may be considered as second-generation expert systems,
or because they try to solve similar problems.

ESPRIT project 387 'KRITIC', even though mainly targeted for ES
tools development for applications in real time, includes the development of
two systems, one for fault diagnosis on telephone switching systems and the
other for load management in electrical power networks. Demonstration
prototypes of both systems were presented in 1987 (ESPRIT, 1987).

Control Data Corporation and Northern States Power Company (Min-
neapolis, MN) are developing an ES prototype for alarm analysis to be used
in NSP's power network, scheduled for mid-1986 (Larson *et al.*, 1985).

Some other real-time applications of ESs have been developed, such
as a chemical plant control system developed by Lockheed-Georgia (Evers
et al., 1984), the EXTASE alarm processing system developed by Labora-
toires de Marcoussis (Jacob *et al.*, 1986), or Carnegie–Mellon's 'Operator
Assistant' and SMOKEY (Talukdar *et al.*, 1986; Carbonell, 1986).

2.   OVERVIEW OF THE CONTROL DISPATCH SYSTEM

IBERDUERO is an electric utility with up to 6500 MW generation capability, covering an area of about 125 000 square kilometres in northern and
central Spain. The operation of the network is controlled from Central
Dispatching equipped with an energy management system that was put into
full operation in mid-1982. In its present state, it handles over 20 000 status
points, 2500 analogue values and 300 accumulators, received either directly
or through two dependent Regional Centres. The information received
includes not only breaker positions, switches and other information
common in every control centre, but also a large amount of protective relay
information (averaging about five statuses for every breaker) and measurements. These protection operation signals are not presented to the dispatchers on the CRTs by means of alarm lights, but are rather logged along

with the breaker operations in a dedicated logger, which can be looked up by the dispatcher in order to get additional information in the case of a disturbance, and eventually will be analysed by protective maintenance personnel.

The experience after four years of the Central Dispatch System operation, even though very positive, has allowed the following problems to be detected:

— In case of disturbance, specially when it is an extensive one, the dispatcher is exposed to a large number of messages, which makes it sometimes difficult to understand fully the ultimate reason for the disturbance.

— It has been shown that in particular the protection status received during a disturbance can provide important information that an average dispatcher may overlook, as a result of his limited knowledge of the protection schemes and the exact meaning of the signals being received.

The above considerations have moved IBERDUERO to undertake the development of an ES, external to the main equipment of the Control Centre but receiving the messages printed in the breaker and protection loggers. The ES will analyse these messages, try to draw out as much information as possible that may help the dispatcher in the understanding and correction of the disturbance.

3.   GOALS AND FURTHER DEVELOPMENTS

The development of the LAIDA project is divided into two main phases, initial prototype and final system. Because of the complexity of the problem to be solved, the initial prototype has a limited functionality. Keeping that in mind, this initial prototype tries to accomplish the following tasks:

(1) Detect when a perturbation happens.
(2) Fault location.
(3) Identification of the fault.
(4) Time pursuit of an evolving incident.
(5) Help to the operator.
(6) Post-mortem analysis.

The final system's technical specifications are not yet frozen, but they include:

(1) Handling of several disturbances happening at the same time.
(2) Consistency checking of old hypotheses based on new incoming data.
(3) Time pursuit of several simultaneous incidents.
(4) Scheduling of the network's full recovery after a fault.

The final system's development is divided into two phases also:

— A second prototype including the first three mentioned issues, in which the reliability of the system's advice is expected to improve by incorporating deep knowledge and the modelling of the network.

— A third prototype which will try to schedule the network's recovery after a fault, which involves hard research topics.

4. FIRST PROTOTYPE DESCRIPTION

4.1 Implementation

There are several ways in which an ES may be added to an existing data processing system. The most appealing one was to build an embedded ES, but this option was unfeasible owing to the nature of the existing SCADA computer system. Therefore we decided to introduce a new computer with the ES running on it, and linked with the SCADA through a communication line such that the ES gets the alarm messages the operator gets, and sends to the SCADA diagnostic messages that it forwards to the operator on its own screen. This way, the existence of an ES is transparent to the operator except for the fact that higher-level information is available from the SCADA.

4.2 Architecture

As shown in Fig. 1, there are three key points that need our major effort in this project:

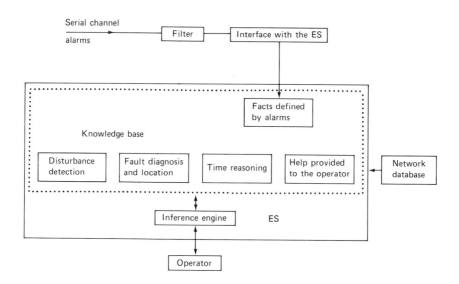

Fig. 1 — ES architecture.

— SCADA–LAIDA interface.
— Data acquisition and filtering.
— Knowledge base development.
Information generated as a consequence of a disturbance in the electrical network is collected by the SCADA system and transmitted to the ES in printer format through an asynchronous line.

The dataflow diagram, in Fig. 2, shows the different modules into which

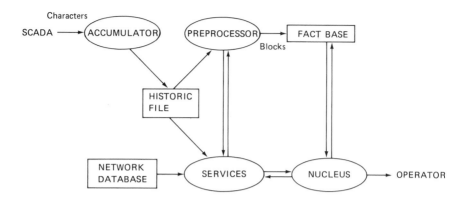

Fig. 2 — Data flow.

the initial prototype is architecturally divided. Each module's tasks are as follows,

— Monitor: makes the system work in a closed loop, activating one module or the other.
— Accumulator: packs characters received from the SCADA system into lines (or alarm messages).
— Preprocessor: eliminates the uninteresting, repeated and redundant alarm messages. It joins alarm messages in blocks of related messages, and analyses the possible relations between successive blocks. Whenever it completes a block, it calls the nucleus for its processing. It identifies and associates lines, substations, etc.
— Nucleus: this is the main part of the ES, and the one that performs the tasks of a higher level of abstraction. It is made of an inference engine and a knowledge base, and it is built using special tools for the design of ES.
— Services: this handles the interface of the nucleus with the static database of the net, as well as some other useful operations that are either difficult to implement with the tool selected, or would be very expensive in execution at run-time.

4.3   Knowledge base
LAIDA is a rule-based ES that monitors an electrical network in a closed loop. It is a shallow-knowledge ES since it is based on symptom–disease associations; this first prototype does not include any model of the network.

The system is able to follow disturbances with time, taking into account new incoming information and, therefore, modifying its first conclusions. It also determines when a disturbance is over, closing it and waiting for a new one.

LAIDA bases its reasoning on the presence (or lack) of alarm messages showing the firing of protections, breakers, etc., which add or remove certainty to several possible hypotheses.

The knowledge base is divided into four main sections:
— The first one generates the possible hypotheses for the location of the fault.
— The second one makes a detailed analysis of the most promising hypotheses in order to select one as the location of the fault.
— The third section explains its reasoning process.
— The fourth one helps the operator, showing the state in which the affected elements were left.

The network's dispatchers are most interested in knowing where a fault has happened, in order to isolate the faulty element and restore the service; this is therefore the issue on which we have spent our main effort. In order to locate a fault, the ES must be able to distinguish between the alarms transmitted at the moment when the fault takes place from those produced as a consequence of subsequent overloads within the system.

Alarm messages are packed in ± 10 second blocks, this number coming from a worst-case estimate of scan plus transmission delay of a message sent from any remote substation; in this way we start a diagnosis attempt with a substantial amount of information which is enough in many cases to locate the origin of a fault. Blocks are examined to check whether they belong to the current fault or to some other one; all alarm messages in a block are assumed to be caused by the same fault.

5.   DEVELOPMENT PROCESS

Knowledge acquisition is the single most important aspect of an ES development, and usually never ends. We had three kinds of experts available for this purpose:
— Energy management system (EMS) experts.
— Experts on protection schemes.
— Dispatchers.

Even though our first choice was to use an ES-building shell, we developed a small sample system using Prolog, and found it unsuitable for our application; from this experience we found that Prolog has a significant speed advantage over a shell, but a disadvantage in its difficulty for the representation of knowledge.

After about a month of knowledge base development using the shell, we decided to change the method of representation we were using, which was based on an attempt to model the possible faults and to identify which signals characterize each one; this mechanism is suitable for research studies on nice and regular networks but hardly so for real systems, which are never nice and regular; therefore we started to use a new method of reasoning based on accumulation of evidence.

For debugging purposes we built two different tools,
— A SCADA emulator, based on a PC with a communications line, with which we sent alarm messages to the system running the ES; the alarm messages were either real ones recorded at the Dispatch Centre or older ones from IBERDUERO's history files:

— A simulator built in the real EMS, for which we created a dummy subnetwork on which we could create faults at will; since the EMS did not know these were test faults, we had to tell the dispatchers to disregard them.

From the history files, IBERDUERO selected 50 significant disturbances which were the base for the system's debug process. After testing and fixing implementation errors in the laboratory, we spent a full month with dispatchers and experts different from the ones involved in the development process trying to identify errors and their causes; we found about 30% of errors, half of which corresponded to faults which had not been considered for the prototype, and identified 44 improvements, most of which were implemented, leaving the remainder for further prototypes.

The system has been installed on-line, and the rest of the debugging process is proceeding slowly, since the rate at which faults happen in the network is slow (about one a day). Both alarm messages and system responses are recorded for later study; weekly meetings are scheduled in order to evaluate the previous week's system performance.

This prototype of LAIDA has been developed by a team of six people, some of them only part-time, in eight months, and has involved about three man-years of effort.

6.   CONCLUSIONS

Several main topics have been identified as being important research issues requiring solution when one tries to develop real-time systems,
— Time-dependent reasoning. New incoming information should be added in real time to the ongoing reasoning process, because it may lead to the validation or refutation of previously-generated hypotheses. The problem cannot be frozen at some instant, but must be analysed in a dynamic fashion. Messages produced by previous protective actions must be identified, as well as their dependency.
— Real-time reasoning. An ES diagnosis must always be available in time to be used effectively; in some cases even hard real-time problems may arise, requiring some answer at a specific moment.
— Knowledge representation. Traditional rule-based knowledge representation may not be sufficient in many cases, therefore requiring a reasoning based on the working principles of the system, involving deep reasoning or even modelling.

This prototype behaves fairly well at diagnosing alarms, even though it has no model or topology of the net available.

Some of the subsequent work on this project, with descriptions that go into more technical detail about the behaviour of the power networks, has been presented elsewhere by Emaldi et al. (1988).

REFERENCES

Carbonell, J. G. (1986) The SMOKEY project: an intelligent sensor-based fireman's assistant. *CMU-CS Internal Paper*, 28 April.

Emaldi, M., Laresgoiti, J., Pérez, J., Amantegui, J., and Echávarri, J. (1988) *Proc. Symposium on Expert Systems Application to Power Systems,* Stockholm and Helsinki, **4,** 32–39.

ESPRIT (1987) *ESPRIT Project 387, Knowledge Representation and Inference Techniques in Industrial Control,* Commission of the European Communities, Brussels, Belgium.

Evers, Smith and Staron (1984) Interfacing an intelligent decision-maker to a real time control system. *SPIE* **485,** 60–64.

Goiricelaya, Emaldi, Echávarri and Amantegui (1987) LAIDA: an expert system for analyzing faults generated in electrical nets. *Proc. 87 ISA Mid-America Conf., March, Chicago,* pp. 223–228.

Jacob, Suslenschi and Vernet (1986) EXTASE: an expert system for alarm processing in process control. *Proc. of ECAI-86,* Vol. 2, p. 103.

Larson, Wollenberg *et al.* (1985) The NSP intelligent alarm processor project. *Proc. of PICA-85.*

Shortliffe, E. H. (1976) *Computer-based Medical Consultations: MYCIN,* Elsevier Computer Science Library.

Smith, R., and Baker (1983) The dipmeter advisor system. *Proc. of 8th IJCAI, Karlsruhe,* pp. 122–179.

Talukdar, Cardozo and Leao (1986) 'TOAST: the power system operator's assistant. *IEEE Computer,* (July) 53–60.

Wittig, T. (1987) Expert systems for real-time applications. *Seminar on Expert Systems, Menendez Pelayo Int. Univ., Santander, July.*

10

AIDA: A declarative language for real-time applications

B. Schnetzler
Institut National de Recherche sur les Transports et leur Sécurité, Centre Informatique Recherche, 2 av du Général Malleret-Joinville, BP 34, 94114 Arcueil Cedex, France

1. INTRODUCTION

The design of an inference engine for general purposes imposes compromises between functions required by artificial intelligence (AI), constraints associated with software architecture and the user's needs.

These compromises are dealt with by means of the realization of the prototype of a **data processing** tool for realizing declarative programming. We sought for a solution implementing a strict minimum of functions; on the the basis of this core, each application (expert system) should be able to **program** its own strategies and construct its own data model. The language interpreted, based on second-order logic, has the level of an **assembly language** (declarative language).

On the basis of an application of the development of an expert system (Forasté and Scemama, 1987), three versions of the inference engine have been developed during the last two years leading to this presentation, written in the Ada language (8000 lines) on an Apollo DN3000 (Schnetzler, 1987c).

2. GENERAL ARCHITECTURE

2.1 Basic concepts

From the very beginning, we chose an integration into conventional data processing in the techniques of realization (Ada, multi-task architecture, etc.) as well as in the functions offered by the inference engine (evaluation of rules in parallel, sharing of resources, etc.). We tried to reproduce in the proposed architecture concepts already well known in data processing: **address**, **process**, ... Each time a known data processing term appears, it has a meaning close to its original signification.

The language is built on the following bases:

— production rules in second-order logic (the attributes may be quantified).
— semi-unification mechanism.
— notion of context (partitioning of a rule base).
— manipulated formalism: the triplet ⟨**address, attribute, value**⟩.

2.2   Basic formalism

The expression of knowledge is made on the basis of the formalism <**address, attribute, value**>. Such a triplet is called a **fact**. It is possible to reduce any data model to a set of triplets.

Example:

STUDENT (card-number *, family-name, first-name)

17311   Dupond   Jack

A *n*-relation is transformed into *n* binary relations associating with each multiplet an **address** forming the link between all the attributes of the mutliplet.

S1,   card-number,   17311
$1,   family-name,   Dupond
$1,   first-name,   Jack

The triplets are stored in an associative memory management unit (AMMU). Each **code** (triplet item) has a semantics that is either directly accessible (an integer, a real, etc.) or known only to the designer of the application (an identifier designing an attribute). In this second case, the **code** corresponds to a reference in a dictionary used only for the dialogue between the software and the user (the software has no control over the semantics of a code in the dictionary).

This representation allows us to give a field format (64 bits) to a code: a description indicator of the type (tag), and a field characterizing the semantics (32 to 48 bits: integer, floating point real, address, time, etc.).

2.3   Time logic

Today, time orientation is indispensable in the design of databases (or expert systems). Time management must not be an added function; it must be taken into account from the very beginning (Ariav, 1987).

The non-monotonicity in logic appears with the introduction of time. In reality, there is non-monotonicity only on the surface. The physical reality is the **event**, and the fact is a quintuplet.

Example:

Change of age at date of birthday:

$1,   age,   22, 13March1986,   ˜create
$1,   age,   22, 13March1987,   ˜delete
$1,   age,   23, 13March1987,   ˜create

So the user reasons in a non-monotonic logic by means of **interpretation** of the contents of the memory (with pre-programmed functions in the engine), but the basic logic functioning is a **monotonic logic**.

For practical reasons, the formalism of the quintuplet has become still richer with a sixth field containing the **inference number**. This number (given automatically by the inference engine) allow us to know at what time and by whom (by what rule) a fact has been deduced. It corresponds to a physical date, while the date introduced earlier has a logical meaning and is accessible whenever the user wants it. The associative memory also offers a notion of **view**: it is possible to ask for information retrieval not to take into account some sextuplets as a function of their inference numbers.

Three directions for use of a memory can be distinguished:

— Information (triplet) retrieval by means of interpretation of the contents of the memory: 'search for Jack's age in May 1986'. We search for the triplet corresponding to the latest creation date preceding the specified date, and for which the deletion date is not at the same time later than the creation date and prior to the specified date.
— Access to raw facts (sextuplets): 'give the list of deductions relating to the rule-choice attribute'. This second use is characteristic of reasoning about reasoning: we try to know how we came to a deduction.
— Information (triplet) retrieval using the **view** mechanism (reasoning with hypotheses): the view is obtained by means of a meta-theory deciding the exclusion of some deductions (each fact can be connected to the trigger action, and rule, that produced it).

2.4   Memory management

For an application having a continuous functioning in the framework of a monotonic logic, there is no general solution for the garbage-collector problem. A piece of information (triplet) ceasing to be of interest because it has become obsolete keeps all its value (sextuplet) for a more complex reasoning at the meta-knowledge (explanation of reasoning, learning, etc.) level. Only the application at the highest level of rights can decide to undertake this meaningless operation: the garbage collector! This can be done in two ways:

— recovery of facts coming from specific inferences (invalidated hypotheses, etc.);
— elimination of obsolete facts up to a given date (creations followed by deletions, and vice versa).

2.5   Architecture

The software was built around some functions realized by Ada tasks:

— n associative memories (in order to access a fact we need a seventh field, indicating in what physical **segment** it is);
— n **processes** (Ada tasks) allowing a rule to be evaluated and running in parallel;

— a **monitoring** task in charge of rule scheduling and resource management;
— a task managing the **background** of the deductions (rule inferences, monitor decisions, external data acquisition) and of their dependences.

2.6   General functioning

The **monitor** has three functions:

— rule scheduling in a **process**.
— resource management (**processors, AMMU**, etc.).
— **interruption** management and process commutation.

A **processor** is an Ada task having its own local memory receiving as a parameter a 4 KB Ada record (a rule) and evaluating it using the associative memories listed by the rule. Each triggering action gives rise to the memorization in the background of a certain number of characteristic pieces of information.

3.   RULE EVALUATION MECHANISM

3.1   Antecedents

One distinguishes among three types of antecedents: **premises, texts** and **conditions**. A **premise** is an access filter (triplet or sextuplet) to an associative memory. A **text** is a function characterized by a certain number of ('in'-mode) parameters and an output result. The parameters are codes. A **condition** is a lexical identity or non-identity operator.

Example:

On the basis of the antecedent 'age (!x) $>=$ 18', in which '!x' is a universally quantified variable, the compiler generates the following antecedents:

age (!x) = ?rg1	$--$ premise
?rg2 $<--$ greater-than-or-equal [rg1, 18]	$--$ text
= (?rg2, &true)	$--$ condition

The notation of a premise is 'attribute (address) = value'. The symbols '?rg1' and '?rg2' indicate existentially quantified variables. The symbol '&true' indicates the 'true' boolean constant. The symbol 'greater-than-or-equal' indicates a function, the result of which is a boolean variable.

The antecedent part of a rule is composed of zero or one **set of positive antecedents** and of zero or n **sets of negative antecedents**.

Example:

Conditions of selection of a route for a vehicle carrying hazardous substances

{ destination (!v) = !d

origin (!v) = ?o
category (vehicle-load (!v)) = hazardous-substances
section-end (!r) = ?o
section-end (!r) = !d }
not { passing-through-built-up-area (!r) = ?a }
not { landscape-site (close-reserve (!r)) = water }

For each premise we add a universally quantified variable which contains, at evaluation time, the segment identifier.

3.2   The unification process
The originality of the unification process, which has borrowed its principles from the SNARK engine (Laurière, 1986), consists of two points:

— dynamic organization of the order of evaluating antecedents;
— evaluation (in the default mode) by saturation of a rule: all the trigger actions of a rule are realized before passing on to the following one.
  The general algorithm is discussed in detail in Schnetzler (1987a).

3.3   Internal structure of a rule
Recording take place in three parts:

— antecedents;
— consequents;
— registers: a register (128 in all) corresponds to each code (constant) of the rule and to each variable. Each instruction (premise, text, condition, consequent instruction) has only registers as parameters.

This representation offers three advantages:

— The dynamic organization of antecedents uses **masks** determining the state of the registers in order to know when an antecedent can be evaluated.
— The unification process does not recognise any major difference between a register created by the compiler (a constant) and a variable. So it is possible for the **monitor** to assign variables before passing over the data structures to the **processor**.
— The feasible 'instructions' are separated from the actual data.

It is possible to share one rule among several **processes**, each of these having its own set of registers. All the evaluation parameters of a rule, including the set of registers, are called the **modality**. The mechanism of previous assignment (pre-assignment) and of **modality** form the bases:

— of the data-processing sharing of **programs**. In particular, two users can apply the same rule to two different physical segments (the monitoring is in charge of linking, according to the context, at the loading of the rule);
— of a finer inference control. The mechanism of pre-assignment is accessible to the user.

3.4   Time processing
The table of the instantaneous state of all the universally quantified variables of a rule forms the **key** of a trigger action. The inference engine ensures the uniqueness of a trigger action. We use this mechanism in order to distinguish the rules according to which they are or are not to give rise to new trigger actions in time, for the same instantaneous values of variables. To each premise (triplet), we add a variable (universally or existentially quantified according to the type of rule) receiving the date of the fact having served the unification (thus the time is introduced (or not) into the **key**).

4.   THE MONITOR
This works according to the following cycle:

— filtering of interruption and commutation of **processes.**
— choice of a **request** (**rule** or **procedure**) for the **active process.**
— activation of the **request**.

All the tasks necessary for the functioning of the system (loading of associative memories, loading of rules, etc.) are made inside this cycle.

4.1   Filtering
Filtering has two functions:

— management of **interruptions** (facts coming from inside and outside).
— recovery of **messages**.

Unlike interruptions of a microprocessor, priorities are not given to facts but to the filters. Thus one fact can generate several interruptions, each one belonging to a different process. An **interruption** can result in either an immediate execution of a procedure by the monitor or just changing the state of a process from waiting to ready.

4.2   Process management
We choose to take over the control structure of conventional data processing: **process, stack, context (procedure), rule (instruction)**, etc. This choice was imposed for reasons of formalism (notion of process) and user-friendliness. The dynamic organization is maintained in a context: the monitor chooses a candidate rule according to its **eligibility** (calculated by the monitor) and its **advisability** (determinated with meta-knowledge, by the expert system).

4.3   Management of several processes
At a given moment, several processes can be running on several processors, but just one process is active on the monitor. The active process is the highest-priority process that it is possible to run (and not yet running on a processor). If the application writes its own operating system (a process) it can manage, with use of priority and interruptions, a more sophisticated scheduling.

The parallel evaluation of rules imposes a verification of non-competition in the access to associative memories. Each request **locks** the memories to which it accedes by means of an access matrix composed of triplets $\langle$base, attribute, access mode$\rangle$. In case of competition, the monitor starts another cycle. The process goes onto the waiting list of resources and remains active on the monitor as long as no higher priority process becomes active.

4.4 Messages
For each action that a rule cannot take immediately, it transmits a message to the monitor by means of creation of facts directly in the background. These are filtered by the monitor, interpreted and translated into parameters of a **procedure** executed later on by the monitor in the context of a process that can be other than the transmitter process.

This mechanism is essential for two reasons:

— access to data used by the monitor (since the monitor must not be blocked, it cannot share its memory).
— verification of rights to realizing certain functions (garbage collector, etc.).

5. BACKGROUND

Part of the functioning of the inference engine consists of memorizing and structuring information, allowing the chaining of the deductions and **dependencies** to be found (Schnetzler, 1987b). The background function is of prime importance, for it alone allows the system to be able to observe its behaviour afterwards.

The background also ensures the attribution of the inference numbers and thus an order of trigger actions.

6. CONCLUSION
The language developed does not offer to the user any of the functions of the development cores of expert systems but, as a counterpart, it allows the exact programming that is desired with otherwise inaccessible performance data.

REFERENCES

Ariav, G. (1987) Design requirements for temporally oriented information systems. *Temporal Aspects in Information Systems, Sophia Antipolis, May 1987.*

Forasté, B. and Scemama, G. (1987) Expert system contribution for control systems: the traffic case. *IMACS, Barcelona, June 1987.*

Laurière, J. L. (1986) 'Un langage déclaratif: SNARK. *Techniques et Sciences Informatiques*, **5** (3).

Schnetzler, B. (1987a) Unification dans une logique non monotone. INRETS, *Note Technique CIR.*

Schnetzler, B. (1987b) Dépendances dans le raisonnement. INRETS, *Note Technique CIR.*

Schnetzler, B. (1987c) AIDA: un langage déclaratif pour l'intelligence artificielle. INRETS, *Rapport de Recherche* (to be published).

Index